AN ESSAY ON THE NATURE AND
SIGNIFICANCE OF ECONOMIC SCIENCE

AN ESSAY ON THE NATURE & SIGNIFICANCE OF ECONOMIC SCIENCE

BY

LIONEL ROBBINS

Professor of Economics in the University of London

SECOND EDITION, REVISED AND EXTENDED

MACMILLAN AND CO., LIMITED
ST. MARTIN'S STREET, LONDON
1952

TO MY FATHER

PREFACE TO THE SECOND EDITION

THE first edition of this essay has been out of print for some time, but apparently some demand for it continues. I have therefore taken advantage of the publisher's decision to reprint to introduce certain alterations and improvements which experience since it was first written seemed to make desirable.

In making these revisions I have not found it necessary to change substantially the main trend of the argument. Public criticism has tended to focus upon the denial in Chapter VI. of the scientific legitimacy of interpersonal comparisons of utility. I am afraid that without the least disposition to be intransigent, here or elsewhere, I am still quite unconvinced. I contended that the aggregation or comparison of the different satisfactions of different individuals involves judgments of value rather than judgments of fact, and that such judgments are beyond the scope of positive science. Nothing that has been said by any of my critics has persuaded me that this contention is false. Beyond a few supplementary remarks intended to elucidate matters further, therefore, I have left this section unaltered. I hope that my critics (some of whom seemed to assume that I was a very combative fellow indeed) will not regard this as a gesture of unfriendly defiance. I assure them I am not at all cocksure about any of my own ideas. But, in spite of the disposition of some of them to refer to this and other well-known propositions as

"Robbinsian Economics," it is not my own, and the weight of the authorities by whom it has been propounded encourages me to believe that in this case, at least, my own lights have not led me astray.

On the other hand, many of my critics have inferred from my arguments in this connection certain precepts of practice which I should be the first to repudiate. It has been held that because I attempted clearly to delimit the spheres of Economics and other social sciences, and Economics and moral philosophy, that therefore I advocated the abstention of the economist from all interest or activity outside his own subject. It has been held—in spite of activities which I feared had become notorious—that I had urged that economists should play no part in shaping the conduct of affairs beyond giving a very prim and restrained diagnosis of the implications of all possible courses of action. My friend Mr. Lindley Fraser was even led to urge upon me in an article entitled "How do we want Economists to Behave?" more socially-minded behaviour. Where so many have misapprehended my intentions, I cannot flatter myself that I was free from obscurity. But I do plead that I did in fact state the contrary—as I thought, most emphatically. In a footnote to Section 6, Chapter V., I stated, "It is more accuracy in mode of statement, not over-austerity in speculative range, for which I am pleading", and I went on to urge that economists have probably high differential advantages as sociologists. And in Section 4, Chapter VI., I went on to say: "All this is not to say that economists should not deliver themselves on ethical questions, any more than an argument that botany is not æsthetics is to say that botanists should not have views of their own on the lay-out of gardens. On the contrary, it is greatly to be desired that economists should have speculated long and widely on these matters, since only in this way will they be in a position to appreciate the implications as regards *given* ends of problems which are put to them for solution." I can only add to this that I quite agree with Mr. Fraser that an economist who is only an economist and who does not happen to be a genius at his subject—and how unwise it is for any of us to assume that we are that—is a pretty poor fish. I agree, too, that by itself Economics affords no solution to any of the important problems of life. I agree that for this reason an education which consists of Economics alone is a very imperfect education. I have taught so long in institutions where this is regarded as a pedagogic axiom that any omission on my part to emphasise it further is to be attributed to the fact that I assumed that everybody would take it for granted. All that I contend is that there is much to be said for separating out the different kinds of propositions involved by the different disciplines which are germane to social action, in order that we may know at each step exactly on what grounds we are deciding. I do not believe that Mr. Fraser really disagrees with me here.

In exactly the same way I would plead that it is a complete misunderstanding of my position to contend that because I have emphasised the conventional nature of the assumptions underlying many of the so-called "measurements" of economic phenomena, I am therefore "opposed" to the carrying out of operations of this sort. It does seem to me to be a matter of great importance to recognise very clearly that in computing such aggregates as the national income or the national capital we are making assumptions which are not reached by scientific analysis, but which are essentially conventional in character. But, as I urged in the body of the essay (pp. 57 and 62), this is not in the least to say that, provided we are fully conscious of the implications of our procedure, there is any objection to such computations. On the contrary, it is clear that not enough of this sort of thing has been done in the past, and that much is to be expected from its extension in the future. Recognition of this, however, is not incompatible with the view that it is desirable to know at each step where we are merely recording facts, and where we are evaluating these facts by arbitrary measures, and it is just because these things are so frequently confused that I still maintain that emphasis on their dissimilarity is not uncalled for.

There is, however, a part of the essay where revision has seemed to be much more incumbent. I have never been satisfied with the chapter on the nature of economic generalisations. I am not conscious of any fundamental change of opinion on these matters. But I do think that in my eagerness to bring out as vividly as possible the significance of certain recent innovations I was led in certain places to a simplification of emphasis and to a looseness in the use of logical terms, apt to be misleading outside the context of my own thought: and the fact that, while some critics have reproached me with "barren scholasticism", others have accused me of "behaviourism", has not permitted me completely to comfort myself with the belief that I elucidated satisfactorily the correct position between these extremes. Accordingly I have rewritten large parts of this chapter, and I have also extended its scope to cover certain more complex topics, such as the meaning of the assumption of purely rational conduct, which, in the earlier version, I had omitted in order not to overload the exposition. I am afraid this makes this part of the book at once more difficult and more contentious. But although I am acutely aware of its imperfections, it satisfies my conscience more than my earlier attempt to deal with such matters only by implication. The opening section of Chapter V. has also been rewritten, and I have introduced additional paragraphs in Section 2, in which I develop a little further my reasons for believing the importance of the contrast between the qualitative laws discussed in the preceding chapter and the quantitative "laws" of statistical analysis. I have also added short sections in Chapters IV. and V. dealing with the relations between statics and dynamics and the possibility of a theory of economic development— matters upon which there seems to exist some unnecessary confusion. I hope that the changes I have made will be acceptable to my friends Professor F. A. von Hayek, Dr. P. N. Rosenstein Rodan and Dr. A. W. Stonier, whose advice and criticisms on these difficult matters have taught me much. They naturally are not responsible for any mistakes which may have crept in.

I have wondered very much what I ought to do about the various attacks on my work which have been made by Professor R. W. Souter. I have read Professor Souter's strictures with interest and respect. As I have said already, I am not convinced by anything that he says about what he calls the "positivism" of my attitude. So far as this part of his case is concerned Professor Souter must demolish, not me, but

Max Weber: and I think Max Weber still stands. But with much of what he says, particularly with regard to the desirability of transcending the rather trite generalisations of elementary statics, I am in cordial agreement. Where I part company with him is in the belief that it is possible to do this without sacrificing precision and without regarding the essential static foundations as useless. My acquaintance with the findings of modern mathematical physics and astronomy is not great, but I question whether the eminent scientists to whom he makes appeal would share his apparently very low opinion of the methods of mathematical economics, however much they felt that its results were still in a very elementary stage. In this respect I am in fairly complete agreement with what has been said already by Professor Knight.[1] I cannot help feeling, too, that, so far as this essay is concerned, one or two inadvertent acerbities of exposition have so angered Professor Souter that he has really misunderstood my position much more than would otherwise have been the case. I regret this, but it is difficult to know what to do about it. At one or two points I have tried to make things clearer. But to defend myself against all these misunderstandings would involve so great an overloading with personal apologia of what is perhaps already an unduly protracted essay that I fear I should become totally unreadable. I do not wish to appear discourteous, and I hope, if time permits me to complete various works now projected, to be able to do something to persuade Professor Souter that my claim that he has misunderstood me is not unjustified.

[1] "Economic Science in Recent Discussion", *American Economic Review*, vol. xxiv., pp. 225-238.

For the rest I have made only small changes. I have deleted certain footnotes whose topical relevance has waned, and I have endeavoured to eliminate certain manifestations of high spirits no longer in harmony with present moods. But nothing short of complete rewriting could conceal the fact that, for better or worse, the essay was written some time ago—large parts of it were conceived and drafted years before publication—and although I think it is perhaps worth reprinting, I do not think it is worth the time that that would involve. So with all the crudities and angularities that remain I commend it once more to the mercies of its readers.

LIONEL ROBBINS.

THE LONDON SCHOOL OF ECONOMICS,
May, 1935.

PREFACE TO THE FIRST EDITION

THE purpose of this essay is twofold. In the first place, it seeks to arrive at precise notions concerning the subject-matter of Economic Science and the nature of the generalisations of which Economic Science consists. Secondly it attempts to explain the limitations and the significance of these generalisations, both as a guide to the interpretation of reality and as a basis for political practice. At the present day, as a result of the theoretical developments of the last sixty years, there is no longer any ground for serious differences of opinion on these matters, once the issues are clearly stated. Yet, for lack of such statement, confusion still persists in many quarters, and false ideas are prevalent with regard to the preoccupations of the economist and the nature and the extent of his competence. As a result, the reputation of Economics suffers, and full advantage is not taken of the knowledge it confers. This essay is an attempt to remedy this deficiency—to make clear what it is that economists discuss and what may legitimately be expected as a result of their discussions. Thus on the one hand it may be regarded as a commentary on the methods and assumptions of pure theory: on the other hand, as a series of prolegomena to work in Applied Economics.

The object of the essay necessitates the taking of broad views. But my aim throughout has been to keep as close to earth as possible. I have eschewed philosophical refinements as falling outside the province in which I have any claim to professional competence; and I have based my propositions on the actual practice of the best modern works on the subject. In a study of this sort, written by an economist for fellow-economists, it seemed better to try to drive home the argument by continual reference to accepted solutions of particular problems, than to elaborate, out of the void, a theory of what Economics should become. At the same time, I have tried to be brief. My object has been to suggest a point of view rather than to treat the subject in all its details. To do this it seemed desirable to be concise even at the expense of sacrificing much material which I had originally collected. I hope, however, at a later stage to publish a work on general Economic Theory in which the principles here laid down are further illustrated and amplified.

For the views which I have advanced, I make no claim whatever to originality. I venture to hope that in one or two instances I have succeeded in giving expository force to certain principles not always clearly stated. But, in the main, my object has been to state, as simply as I could, propositions which are the common property of most modern economists. I owe much to conversations with my colleagues and pupils at the School of Economics. For the rest I have acknowledged in footnotes the debts of which I am chiefly conscious. I should like, however, once more to acknowledge my especial indebtedness to the works of Professor Ludwig von Mises and to the *Commonsense of Political Economy* of the late Philip Wicksteed. The considerable extent to which I have cited these sources is yet a very inadequate reflection of the general assistance which I have derived from their use.

LIONEL ROBBINS.

THE LONDON SCHOOL OF ECONOMICS,
February, 1932.

CONTENTS

CHAPTER IV

CHAPTER V

CHAPTER VI

CHAPTER I

THE SUBJECT-MATTER OF ECONOMICS

1. THE object of this Essay is to exhibit the nature and significance of Economic Science. Its first task therefore is to delimit the subject-matter of Economics —to provide a working definition of what Economics is about.

Unfortunately, this is by no means as simple as it sounds. The efforts of economists during the last hundred and fifty years have resulted in the establishment of a body of generalisations whose substantial accuracy and importance are open to question only by the ignorant or the perverse. But they have achieved no unanimity concerning the ultimate nature of the common subject-matter of these generalisations. The central chapters of the standard works on Economics retail, with only minor variations, the main principles of the science. But the chapters in which the object of the work is explained still present wide divergences. We all talk about the same things, but we have not yet agreed what it is we are talking about.[1]

---

[1] Lest this should be thought an overstatement I subjoin below a few characteristic definitions. I have confined my choice to Anglo-Saxon literature because, as will be shown later on, a more satisfactory state of affairs is coming to prevail elsewhere. "Economics is a study of mankind in the ordinary business of life; it examines that part of individual and social action which is most closely connected with the attainment and with the use of the material requisites of well-being" (Marshall, *Principles*, p. 1).

This is not in any way an unexpected or a disgraceful circumstance. As Mill pointed out a hundred years ago, the definition of a science has almost invariably, not preceded, but followed the creation of the science itself. "Like the wall of a city it has usually been erected, not to be a receptacle for such edifices as might afterwards spring up, but to circumscribe an aggregate already in existence."[1] Indeed, it follows from the very nature of a science that until it has reached a certain stage of development, definition of its scope is necessarily impossible. For the unity of a science only shows itself in the unity of the problems it is able to solve, and such unity is not discovered until the interconnection of its explanatory principles has been established.[2] Modern Economics takes its rise from various separate spheres of practical and philosophical enquiry—from investigations of the balance of trade—from discussions of the legitimacy of the taking of interest.[3] It was not until quite recent times that it had become sufficiently unified for the

---

"Economics is the science which treats phenomena from the standpoint of price" (Davenport, *Economics of Enterprise*, p. 25). "The aim of Political Economy is the explanation of the general causes on which the material welfare of human beings depends" (Cannan, *Elementary Political Economy*, p. 1) "It is too wide a definition to speak of Economics as the science of the material side of human welfare." Economics is "the study of the general methods by which men co-operate to meet their material needs" (Beveridge, *Economics as a Liberal Education, Economica*, vol. i., p. 3). Economics, according to Professor Pigou, is the study of economic welfare, economic welfare being defined as " that part of welfare which can be brought directly or indirectly into relation with the measuring rod of money" (*Economics of Welfare*, 3rd edition, p. 1). The sequel will show how widely the implications of these definitions diverge from one another.

[1] *Unsettled Questions of Political Economy*, p. 120.

[2] "Nicht die 'sachlichen' Zusammenhänge der 'Dinge' sondern die *gedanklichen* Zusammenhänge der *Probleme* liegen den Arbeitsgebieten der Wissenschaften zugrunde" (Max Weber, *Die Objectivität sozialwissenschaftlicher und sozialpolitischer Erkenntnis, Gesammelte Aufsätze zur Wissenschaftslehre*, p. 166).

[3] See Cannan, *Review of Economic Theory*, pp. 1-35, and Schumpeter, *Epochen der Methoden- und Dogmengeschichte*, pp. 21-38.

identity of the problems underlying these different enquiries to be detected. At an earlier stage, any attempt to discover the ultimate nature of the science was necessarily doomed to disaster. It would have been waste of time to have attempted it.

But once this stage of unification has been reached not only is it not waste of time to attempt precise delimitation; it is waste of time not to do so. Further elaboration can only take place if the objective is clearly indicated. The problems are no longer suggested by naïve reflection. They are indicated by gaps in the unity of theory, by insufficiencies in its explanatory principles. Unless one has grasped what this unity is, one is apt to go off on false scents. There can be little doubt that one of the greatest dangers which beset the modern economist is preoccupation with the irrelevant—the multiplication of activities having little or no connection with the solution of problems strictly germane to his subject.[1] There can be equally little doubt that, in those centres where questions of this sort are on the way to ultimate settlement, the solution of the central theoretical problems proceeds most rapidly. Moreover, if these solutions are to be fruitfully applied, if we are to understand correctly the bearing of Economic Science on practice, it is essential that we should know exactly the implications and limitations of the generalisations it establishes. It is therefore with an easy conscience that we may advance to what, at first sight, is the extremely academic problem of finding a formula to describe the general subject-matter of Economics.

[1] See Chapter II., Section 5, especially the footnote on p. 42, for further elaboration of this point.

2. The definition of Economics which would probably command most adherents, at any rate in Anglo-Saxon countries, is that which relates it to the study of the causes of material welfare. This element is common to the definitions of Cannan[1] and Marshall,[2] and even Pareto, whose approach[3] in so many ways was so different from that of the two English economists, gives it the sanction of his usage. It is implied, too, in the definition of J. B. Clark.[4]

And, at first sight, it must be admitted, it certainly does appear as if we have here a definition which for practical purposes describes the object of our interest. In ordinary speech there is unquestionably a sense in which the word "economic" is used as equivalent to "material". One has only to reflect upon its signification to the layman in such phrases as "Economic History",[5] or "a conflict between economic and political advantage", to realise the extreme plausibility of this interpretation. No doubt there are some matters falling outside this definition which seem to fall within the scope of Economics, but at first sight these may very well seem to be of the order of marginal cases inevitable with every definition.

But the final test of the validity of any such definition is not its apparent harmony with certain usages of everyday speech, but its capacity to describe exactly the ultimate subject-matter of the main

---

[1] *Wealth*, 1st edition, p. 17.

[2] *Principles*, 8th edition, p. 1.

[3] *Cours d'Economie Politique*, p. 6.

[4] *Essentials of Economic Theory*, p. 5. See also *Philosophy of Wealth*, ch. i. In this chapter the difficulties discussed below are explicitly recognised, but, surprisingly enough, instead of this leading to a rejection of the definition, it leads only to a somewhat surprising attempt to change the significance of the word "material".

[5] But see Chapter II. below for an examination of the validity of this interpretation.

generalisations of the science.[1] And when we submit
the definition in question to this test, it is seen to
possess deficiencies which, so far from being marginal
and subsidiary, amount to nothing less than a complete failure to exhibit either the scope or the significance of the most central generalisations of all.

Let us take any one of the main divisions of theoretical Economics and examine to what extent it is covered
by the definition we are examining. We should all
agree, for instance, that a theory of wages was an
integral part of any system of economic analysis. Can
we be content with the assumption that the phenomena
with which such a theory has to deal are adequately
described as pertaining to the more material side of
human welfare?

Wages, in the strict sense of the term, are sums
earned by the performance of work at stipulated rates
under the supervision of an employer. In the looser
sense in which the term is often used in general
economic analysis, it stands for labour incomes other
than profits. Now it is perfectly true that some wages
are the price of work which may be described as conducive to material welfare—the wages of a sewage
collector, for instance. But it is equally true that some

[1] In this connection it is perhaps worth while clearing up a confusion
which not infrequently occurs in discussions of terminology. It is often
urged that scientific definitions of words used both in ordinary language
and in scientific analysis should not depart from the usages of everyday
speech. No doubt this is a counsel of perfection, but in principle the main
contention may be accepted. Great confusion is certainly created when a word
which is used in one sense in business practice is used in another sense in
the analysis of such practice. One has only to think of the difficulties which
have been created by such departures in regard to the meaning of the term
capital. But it is one thing to follow everyday usage when appropriating
a term. It is another thing to contend that everyday speech is the final
court of appeal when defining a science. For in this case the significant
implication of the word *is* the subject-matter of the generalisations of the
science. And it is only by reference to these that the definition can finally
be established. Any other procedure would be intolerable.

wages, the wages of the members of an orchestra, for instance, are paid for work which has not the remotest bearing on material welfare. Yet the one set of services, equally with the other, commands a price and enters into the circle of exchange. The theory of wages is as applicable to the explanation of the latter as it is to the explanation of the former. Its elucidations are not limited to wages which are paid for work ministering to the "more material" side of human well-being—whatever that may be.

Nor is the situation saved if we turn from the work for which wages are paid to the things on which wages are spent. It might be urged that it is not because what the wage-earner produces is conducive to other people's material welfare that the theory of wages may be subsumed under the description, but because what he gets is conducive to his own. But this does not bear examination for an instant. The wage-earner may buy bread with his earnings. But he may buy a seat at the theatre. A theory of wages which ignored all those sums which were paid for "immaterial" services or spent on "immaterial" ends would be in-tolerable. The circle of exchange would be hopelessly ruptured. The whole process of general analysis could never be employed. It is impossible to conceive significant generalisations about a field thus arbitrarily delimited.

It is improbable that any serious economist has attempted to delimit the theory of wages in this manner, however much he may have attempted thus to delimit the whole body of generalisations of which the theory of wages is a part. But attempts have certainly been made to deny the applicability of economic analysis to the examination of the achievement of

ends other than material welfare. No less an economist than Professor Cannan has urged that the
political economy of war is "a contradiction in
terms",[1] apparently on the ground that, since Economics is concerned with the causes of material welfare,
and since war is not a cause of material welfare, war
cannot be part of the subject-matter of Economics.
As a moral judgment on the uses to which abstract
knowledge should be put, Professor Cannan's strictures
may be accepted. But it is abundantly clear, as
Professor Cannan's own practice has shown, that, so
far from Economics having no light to throw on the
successful prosecution of modern warfare, it is highly
doubtful whether the organisers of war can possibly
do without it. It is a curious paradox that Professor
Cannan's pronouncement on this matter should occur
in a work which, more than any other published in
our language, uses the apparatus of economic analysis
to illuminate many of the most urgent and the most
intricate problems of a community organised for war.

This habit on the part of modern English economists
of describing Economics as concerned with the causes
of material welfare, is all the more curious when we
reflect upon the unanimity with which they have
adopted a non-material definition of "productivity".
Adam Smith, it will be remembered, distinguished
between productive and unproductive labour, according as the efforts in question did or did
not result in the production of a tangible material
object. "The labour of some of the most respectable
orders in the society is, like that of menial servants,
unproductive of any value and does not fix or realise
itself in any permanent subject or vendible commodity

---

[1] Cannan. *An Economist's Protest*, p. 49.

which endures after that labour is past. . . . The sovereign, for example, with all the officers both of justice and war who serve under him are unproductive labourers. . . . In the same class must be ranked some both of the gravest and most important, and some of the most frivolous professions: churchmen, lawyers, physicians, men of letters of all kinds; players, buffoons, musicians, opera singers, opera dancers, etc. . . ."[1] Modern economists, Professor Cannan foremost among them,[2] have rejected this conception of productivity as inadequate.[3] So long as it is the object of demand, whether privately or collectively formulated, the labour of the opera singers and dancers must be regarded as "productive". But productive of what? Of material welfare because it cheers the business man and releases new stores of energy to organise the production of material? That way lies dilettantism and *Wortspielerei*. It is productive because it is valued, because it has specific importance for various "economic subjects". So far is modern theory from the point of view of Adam Smith and the Physiocrats that the epithet of productive labour is denied even to the production of material objects, if the material objects are not valuable. Indeed, it has gone further than this. Professor Fisher, among others, has demonstrated conclusively[4] that the income from a material object must in the last resort be conceived as an "immaterial"

---

[1] *Wealth of Nations* (Cannan's ed.), p. 315.

[2] *Theories of Production and Distribution*, pp. 18-31; *Review of Economic Theory*, pp. 49-51.

[3] It is even arguable that the reaction has gone too far. Whatever its demerits, the Smithian classification had a significance for capital theory which in recent times has not always been clearly recognised. See Taussig, *Waaes and Capital*, pp. 132-151.

[4] *The Nature of Capital and Income*, ch. vii.

use. From my house equally as from my valet or the services of the opera singer, I derive an income which "perishes in the moment of its production".

But, if this is so, is it not misleading to go on describing Economics as the study of the causes of material welfare? The services of the opera dancer are wealth. Economics deals with the pricing of these services, equally with the pricing of the services of a cook. Whatever Economics is concerned with, it is *not* concerned with the causes of material welfare as such.

The causes which have led to the persistence of this definition are mainly historical in character. It is the last vestige of Physiocratic influence. English economists are not usually interested in questions of scope and method. In nine cases out of ten where this definition occurs, it has probably been taken over quite uncritically from some earlier work. But, in the case of Professor Cannan, its retention is due to more positive causes; and it is instructive to attempt to trace the processes of reasoning which seem to have rendered it plausible to so penetrating and so acute an intellect.

The rationale of any definition is usually to be found in the use which is actually made of it. Professor Cannan develops his definition in close juxtaposition to a discussion of "the Fundamental Conditions of Wealth for Isolated Man and for Society",[1] and it is in connection with this discussion that he actually uses his conception of what is economic and what is not. It is no accident, it may be suggested, that if the approach to economic analysis is made from this point of view, the "materialist" definition, as we may

[1] This is the title of ch. ii. of *Wealth* (1st edition).

call it, has the maximum plausibility. This deserves vindication in some detail.

Professor Cannan commences by contemplating the activities of a man isolated completely from society and enquiring what conditions will determine his wealth—that is to say, his material welfare. In such conditions, a division of activities into "economic" and "non-economic"—activities directed to the increase of material welfare and activities directed to the increase of non-material welfare —has a certain plausibility. If Robinson Crusoe digs potatoes, he is pursuing material or "economic" welfare. If he talks to the parrot, his activities are "non-economic" in character. There is a difficulty here to which we must return later, but it is clear *prima facie* that, in this context, the distinction is not ridiculous.

But let us suppose Crusoe is rescued and, coming home, goes on the stage and talks to the parrot for a living. Surely in such conditions these conversations have an economic aspect. Whether he spends his earnings on potatoes or philosophy, Crusoe's getting and spending are capable of being exhibited in terms of the fundamental economic categories.

Professor Cannan does not pause to ask whether his distinction is very helpful in the analysis of an exchange economy—though, after all, it is here that economic generalisations have the greatest practical utility. Instead, he proceeds forthwith to consider the "fundamental conditions of wealth" for society considered as a whole irrespective of whether it is organised on the basis of private property and free exchanges or not. And here again his definition becomes plausible: once more the aggregate of social activities can be sorted out into the twofold classification it implies. Some activities are devoted to the pursuit of material welfare: some are not. We think, for instance, of the executive of a communist society, deciding to spend so much labour-time on the provision of bread, so much on the provision of circuses.

But even here and in the earlier case of the Crusoe Economy, the procedure is open to what is surely a crushing objection. Let us accept Professor Cannan's use of the terms "economic" and "non-economic" as being equivalent to conducive to material and non-material welfare respectively. Then we may say with him that the wealth of society will be greater the greater proportion of time which is devoted to material ends, the less the proportion which is devoted to immaterial ends. We may say this. But we must also admit that, using the word "economic" in a perfectly normal sense, there still remains an economic problem, both for society and for the individual, of choosing between these two kinds of activity—a problem of how, given the relative valuations of product and leisure and the opportunities of production, the fixed supply of twenty-four hours in the day is to be divided between them. *There is still an economic problem of deciding between the "economic" and the "non-economic".* One of the main problems of the Theory of Production lies half outside Professor Cannan's definition.

Is not this in itself a sufficient argument for its abandonment?[1]

---

[1] There are other quarrels which we might pick with this particular definition. From the philosophical point of view, the term "material welfare" is a very odd construction. "The material causes of welfare" might be admitted. But "material welfare" seems to involve a division of states of mind which are essentially unitary. For the purposes of this chapter, however, it has seemed better to ignore these deficiencies and to concentrate on the main question, namely, whether the definition can in any way describe the contents of which it is intended to serve as a label.

3. But where, then, are we to turn? The position is by no means hopeless. Our critical examination of the "materialist" definition has brought us to a point from which it is possible to proceed forthwith to formulate a definition which shall be immune from all these strictures.

Let us turn back to the simplest case in which we found this definition inappropriate—the case of isolated man dividing his time between the production of real income and the enjoyment of leisure. We have just seen that such a division may legitimately be said to have an economic aspect. Wherein does this aspect consist?

The answer is to be found in the formulation of the exact conditions which make such division necessary. They are four. In the first place, isolated man wants both real income and leisure. Secondly, he has not enough of either fully to satisfy his want of each. Thirdly, he can spend his time in augmenting his real income or he can spend it in taking more leisure. Fourthly, it may be presumed that, save in most exceptional cases, his want for the different constituents of real income and leisure will be different. Therefore he has to choose. He has to economise. The disposition of his time and his resources has a relationship to his system of wants. It has an economic aspect.

This example is typical of the whole field of economic studies. From the point of view of the economist, the conditions of human existence exhibit four fundamental characteristics. The ends are various. The time and the means for achieving these ends are limited and capable of alternative application. At the same time the ends have different importance. Here we are, sentient creatures with bundles of desires and aspirations, with masses of instinctive tendencies all urging us in different ways to action. But the time in which these tendencies can be expressed is limited. The external world does not offer full opportunities for their complete achievement. Life is short. Nature is niggardly. Our fellows have other objectives. Yet we can use our lives for doing different things, our materials and the services of others for achieving different objectives.

Now *by itself* the multiplicity of ends has no necessary interest for the economist. If I want to do two things, and I have ample time and ample means with which to do them, and I do not want the time or the means for anything else, then my conduct assumes none of those forms which are the subject of economic science. Nirvana is not necessarily single bliss. It is merely the complete satisfaction of *all* requirements.

Nor is the mere limitation of means *by itself* sufficient to give rise to economic phenomena. If means of satisfaction have no alternative use, then they may be scarce, but they cannot be economised. The Manna which fell from heaven may have been scarce, but, if it was impossible to exchange it for something else or to postpone its use,[1] it was not the object of any activity with an economic aspect.

Nor again is the alternative applicability of scarce means a complete condition of the existence of the kind of phenomena we are analysing. If the economic

---

[1] It is perhaps worth emphasising the significance of this qualification. The application of technically similar means to the achievement of qualitatively similar ends *at different times* constitute alternative uses of these means. Unless this is clearly realised, one of the most important types of economic action is overlooked.

subject has two ends and one means of satisfying them, and the two ends are of equal importance, his position will be like the position of the ass in the fable, paralysed halfway between the two equally attractive bundles of hay.[1]

But when time and the means for achieving ends are limited *and* capable of alternative application, *and* the ends are capable of being distinguished in order of importance, then behaviour necessarily assumes the form of choice. Every act which involves time and scarce means for the achievement of one end involves the relinquishment of their use for the achievement of another. It has an economic aspect.[2] If I want bread and sleep, and in the time at my disposal I cannot have all I want of both, then some part of my wants of bread and sleep must go unsatisfied. If, in a limited lifetime, I would wish to be both a philosopher and a mathematician, but my rate of acquisition of knowledge is such that I cannot do both completely, then some part of my wish for philosophical or mathematical competence or both must be relinquished.

Now not all the means for achieving human ends are limited. There are things in the external world which are present in such comparative abundance that the use of particular units for one thing does not

---

[1] This may seem an unnecessary refinement, and in the first edition of this essay I left it out for that reason. But the condition that there exists a hierarchy of ends is so important in the theory of value that it seems better to state it explicitly even at this stage.   See Chapter IV., Section 2.

[2] Cp. Schönfeld, *Grenznutzen und Wirtschaftsrechnung*, p. 1; Hans Mayer, *Untersuchungen zu dem Grundgesetze der wirtschaftlichen Wertrechnung* (*Zeitschrift für Volkswirtschaft und Sozialpolitik*, Bd. 2, p. 123).

It should be sufficiently clear that it is not "time" as such which is scarce, but rather the potentialities of ourselves viewed as instruments. To speak of scarcity of time is simply a metaphorical way of invoking this rather abstract concept.

involve going without other units for others. The air which we breathe, for instance, is such a "free" commodity. Save in very special circumstances, the fact that we need air imposes no sacrifice of time or resources. The loss of one cubic foot of air implies no sacrifice of alternatives. Units of air have no specific significance for conduct. And it is conceivable that living creatures might exist whose "ends" were so limited that all goods for them were "free" goods, that no goods had specific significance.

But, in general, human activity with its multiplicity of objectives has not this independence of time or specific resources. The time at our disposal is limited. There are only twenty-four hours in the day. We have to choose between the different uses to which they may be put. The services which others put at our disposal are limited. The material means of achieving ends are limited. We have been turned out of Paradise. We have neither eternal life nor unlimited means of gratification. Everywhere we turn, if we choose one thing we must relinquish others which, in different circumstances, we would wish not to have relinquished. Scarcity of means to satisfy ends of varying importance is an almost ubiquitous condition of human behaviour.[1]

Here, then, is the unity of subject of Economic Science, the forms assumed by human behaviour in disposing of scarce means. The examples we have

---

[1] It should be clear that there is no disharmony between the conception of end here employed, the terminus of particular lines of conduct in acts of final consumption, and the conception involved when it is said that there is but one end of activity—the maximising of satisfaction, "utility", or what not. Our "ends" are to be regarded as proximate to the achievement of this ultimate end. If the means are scarce they cannot all be achieved, and according to the scarcity of means and their relative importance the achievement of some ends has to be relinquished.

discussed already harmonise perfectly with this conception. Both the services of cooks and the services of opera dancers are limited in relation to demand and can be put to alternative uses. The theory of wages in its entirety is covered by our present definition. So, too, is the political economy of war. The waging of war necessarily involves the withdrawal of scarce goods and services from other uses, if it is to be satisfactorily achieved. It has therefore an economic aspect. The economist studies the disposal of scarce means. He is interested in the way different degrees of scarcity of different goods give rise to different ratios of valuation between them, and he is interested in the way in which changes in conditions of scarcity, whether coming from changes in ends or changes in means—from the demand side or the supply side—affect these ratios. Economics is the science which studies human behaviour as a relationship between ends and scarce means which have alternative uses.[1]

4. It is important at once to notice certain implications of this conception. The conception we have rejected, the conception of Economics as the study of the causes of material welfare, was what may be called a *classificatory* conception. It marks off certain kinds of human behaviour, behaviour directed to the procuring of material welfare, and designates these as the subject-matter of Economics. Other kinds of conduct lie outside the scope of its investigations. The conception we have adopted may be described as *analytical*. It does not attempt to pick out certain

---

‘ Cp. Menger, *Grundsätze der Volkswirtschaftslehre*, 1te Aufl., pp. 51-70; Mises, *Die Gemeinwirtschaft*, pp. 98 *seq.*; Fetter, *Economic Principles*, ch. i.; Strigl, *Die ökonomischen Kategorien und die Organisation der Wirtschaft*, *passim*; Mayer. *op. cit.*

kinds of behaviour, but focuses attention on a particular *aspect* of behaviour, the form imposed by the influence of scarcity.[1] It follows from this, therefore, that in so far as it presents this aspect, any kind of human behaviour falls within the scope of economic generalisations. We do not say that the production of potatoes is economic activity and the production of philosophy is not. We say rather that, in so far as either kind of activity involves the relinquishment of other desired alternatives, it has its economic aspect. There are no limitations on the subject-matter of Economic Science save this.

Certain writers, however, while rejecting the conception of Economics as concerned with material welfare, have sought to impose on its scope a restriction of another nature: They have urged that the behaviour with which Economics is concerned is essentially a certain type of social behaviour, the behaviour implied by the institutions of the Individualist Exchange Economy. On this view, that kind of behaviour which is not specifically social in this definite sense is not the subject-matter of Economics, Professor Amonn in particular has devoted almost infinite pains to elaborating this conception.[2]

Now it may be freely admitted that, within the

---

[1] On the distinction between analytical and classificatory definitions, see Irving Fisher, *Senses of Capital* (*Economic Journal*, vol. vii., p. 213). It is interesting to observe that the change in the conception of Economics implied by our definition is similar to the change in the conception of capital implied in Professor Fisher's definition. Adam Smith defined capital as a kind of wealth. Professor Fisher would have us regard it as an aspect of wealth.

[2] See his *Objekt und Grundbegriffe der theoretischen Nationalökonomie*, 2 Aufl. The criticisms of Schumpeter and Strigl on pp. 110-125 and pp. 155-156 are particularly important from this point of view. With the very greatest respect for Professor Amonn's exhaustive analysis, I cannot resist the impression that he is inclined rather to magnify the degree of his divergence from the attitude of these two authors.

wide field of our definition, the attention of economists
is focused chiefly on the complications of the Exchange
Economy. The reason for this is one of interest. The
activities of isolated man, equally with the activities
of the exchange economy, are subject to the limitations
we are contemplating. But, from the point of view of
isolated man, economic analysis is unnecessary. The
elements of the problem are given to unaided reflection. Examination of the behaviour of a Crusoe may
be immensely illuminating as an aid to more advanced
studies. But, from the point of view of Crusoe, it is
obviously *extra-marginal*. So too in the case of a
"closed" communistic society. Again, from the point
of view of the economist, the comparison of the
phenomena of such a society with those of the exchange economy may be very illuminating. But from
the point of view of the members of the executive,
the generalisations of Economics would be un-
interesting. Their position would be analogous to
Crusoe's. For them the economic problem would
be merely whether to apply productive power to this
or to that. Now, as Professor Mises has emphasised,
given central ownership and control of the means of
production, the registering of individual pulls and
resistances by a mechanism of prices and costs is
excluded by definition. It follows therefore that
the decisions of the executive must necessarily be
"arbitrary".[1] That is to say, they must be based on
its valuations—not on the valuations of consumers
and producers. This at once simplifies the form of
choice. Without the guidance of a price system, the

---

[1] See Mises, *Die Gemeinwirtschaft*, pp. 94-138. In his *Economic Planning
in Soviet Russia*, Professor Boris Brutzkus has well shown the way in which
this difficulty has been exemplified in the various phases of the Russian
experiment.

organisation of production must depend on the valuations of the final organiser, just as the organisation of a patriarchal estate unconnected with a money economy must depend on the valuations of the patriarch.

But in the exchange economy the position is much more complicated. The implications of individual decisions reach beyond the repercussions on the individual. One may realise completely the implications for oneself of a decision to spend money in this way rather than in that way. But it is not so easy to trace the effects of this decision on the whole complex of "scarcity relationships"—on wages, on profits, on prices, on rates of capitalisation, and the organisation of production. On the contrary, the utmost effort of abstract thought is required to devise generalisations which enable us to grasp them. For this reason economic analysis has most utility in the exchange economy. It is unnecessary in the isolated economy. It is debarred from any but the simplest generalisations by the very *raison d'être* of a strictly communist society. But where independent initiative in social relationships is permitted to the individual, there economic analysis comes into its own.

But it is one thing to contend that economic analysis has *most interest and utility* in an exchange economy. It is another to contend that its subject-matter is *limited* to such phenomena. The unjustifiability of this latter contention may be shown conclusively by two considerations. In the first place, it is clear that behaviour outside the exchange economy is conditioned by the same limitation of means in relation to ends as behaviour within the economy, and is capable of being subsumed under the same funda-

mental categories.[1] The generalisations of the theory
of value are as applicable to the behaviour of isolated
man or the executive authority of a communist society,
as to the behaviour of man in an exchange economy—
even if they are not so illuminating in such contexts.
The exchange relationship is a *technical* incident, a
technical incident indeed which gives rise to nearly
all the interesting complications, but still, for all that,
subsidiary to the main fact of scarcity.

In the second place, it is clear that the phenomena
of the exchange economy itself can only be explained
by *going behind* such relationships and invoking the
operation of those laws of choice which are best seen
when contemplating the behaviour of the isolated
individual.[2] Professor Amonn seems willing to admit
that such a system of pure Economics may be useful
as an auxiliary to Economic Science, but he precludes
himself from making it the basis of the main system
by postulating that the subject-matter of Economics
must be defined in terms of the problems discussed by
Ricardo. The view that a definition must describe an
existing body of knowledge and not lay down arbitrary
limits is admirable. But, it may legitimately be asked,
why stop at Ricardo? Is it not clear that the imperfections of the Ricardian system were due to just this
circumstance that it stopped at the valuations of the
market and did not press through to the valuations of
the individual? Surely it is the great achievement of

---

[1] See Strigl, *op. cit.*, pp. 23-28.

[2] Professor Cassel's dismissal of Crusoe Economics (*Fundamental
Thoughts*, p. 27) seems unfortunate since it is only when contemplating
the conditions of isolated man that the importance of the condition that the
scarce means must have alternative uses if there is to be economic activity,
which was emphasised above, leaps clearly to the eye. In a social economy
of any kind, the mere multiplicity of economic subjects leads one to overlook
the possibility of the existence of scarce goods with no alternative uses.

the more recent theories of value to have surmounted just this barrier?[1]

5. Finally, we may return to the definition we rejected and examine how it compares with the definition we have now chosen.

At first sight, it is possible to underestimate the divergence between the two definitions. The one regards the subject-matter of economics as human behaviour conceived as a relationship between ends and means, the other as the causes of material welfare. Scarcity of means and the causes of material welfare—are these not more or less the same thing ?

Such a contention, however, would rest upon a misconception. It is true that the scarcity of materials is one of the limitations of conduct. But the scarcity of our own time and the services of others is just as important. The scarcity of the services of the schoolmaster and the sewage man have each their economic aspect. Only by saying that services are material vibrations or the like can one stretch the definition to cover the whole field. But this is not only perverse, it is also misleading. In this form the definition may *cover* the field, but it does not describe it. For it is not the *materiality* of even material means of gratification

---

[1] The objections outlined above to the definition suggested by Professor Amonn should be sufficient to indicate the nature of the objections to those definitions which run in terms of phenomena from the standpoint of price (Davenport), susceptibility to the "measuring rod of money" (Pigou), or the "science of exchange" (Landry, etc.). Professor Schumpeter, in his *Wesen und Hauptinhalt der theoretischen Nationalökonomie,* has attempted with never to be forgotten subtlety to vindicate the latter definition by demonstrating that it is possible to *conceive* all the fundamental aspects of behaviour germane to Economic Science as having the form of exchange. That this is correct and that it embodies a truth fundamental to the proper understanding of equilibrium theory may be readily admitted. But it is one thing to generalise the notion of exchange as a *construction.* It is another to use it in this sense as a *criterion.* That it *can* function in this way is not disputed. But that it throws the maximum light on the ultimate nature of our subject-matter is surely open to question.

which gives them their status as economic goods; it is their relation to valuations. It is their relationship to given wants rather than their technical substance which is significant. The "materialist" definition of Economics therefore misrepresents the science as we know it. Even if it does not definitely mislead as to its scope, it necessarily fails to convey an adequate concept of its nature. There seems no valid argument against its rejection.

At the same time, it is important to realise that what is rejected is but a definition. We do not reject the body of knowledge which it was intended to describe. The practice of those who have adopted it fits in perfectly with the alternative definition which has been suggested. There is no important generalisation in the whole range of Professor Cannan's system, for instance, which is incompatible with the definition of the subject-matter of Economics in terms of the disposal of scarce means.

Moreover, the very example which Professor Cannan selects to illustrate his definition fits much better into our framework than it does into his. "Economists", he says, "would agree that 'Did Bacon write Shakespeare?' was not an economic question, and that the satisfaction which believers in the cryptogram would feel if it were universally accepted would not be an economic satisfaction. . . . On the other hand, they would agree that the controversy would have an economic side if copyright were perpetual and the descendants of Bacon and Shakespeare were disputing the ownership of the plays."[1] Exactly. But why? Because the ownership of the copyright involves material welfare? But the

---

[1] *Wealth* (1st edition), ch. i.

proceeds may all go to missionary societies. Surely the question has an economic aspect simply and solely because the copyright laws supposed would make the use of the plays scarce in relation to the demand for their use, and would in turn provide their owners with command over scarce means of gratification which otherwise would be differently distributed.

CHAPTER II

ENDS AND MEANS

1. WE have now established a working definition of
the subject-matter of Economics. The next step is to
examine its implications. In this chapter we shall be
concerned with the status of ends and means as they
figure in Economic Theory and Economic History.
In the next we shall be concerned with the interpretation of various economic "quantities".

2. Let us turn first to the status of ends.[1]

Economics, we have seen, is concerned with that
aspect of behaviour which arises from the scarcity of
means to achieve given ends. It follows that Economics
is entirely neutral between ends; that, in so far as the
achievement of *any* end is dependent on scarce means,
it is germane to the preoccupations of the economist.
Economics is not concerned with ends as such. It
assumes that human beings have ends in the sense
that they have tendencies to conduct which can be
defined and understood, and it asks how their
progress towards their objectives is conditioned by
the scarcity of means—how the disposal of the scarce
means is contingent on these ultimate valuations.

It should be clear, therefore, that to speak of any
end as being itself "economic" is entirely misleading.

[1] The following sections are devoted to the elucidation of the implications of Economics as a positive science. On the question whether Economics
should aspire to a normative status, see Chapter VI., Section 4, below.

The habit, prevalent among certain groups of econo-mists, of discussing "economic satisfactions" is alien to the central intention of economic analysis. A satis-faction is to be conceived as an end-product of activity. It is not itself part of that activity which we study. It would be going too far to urge that it is impossible to conceive of "economic satisfactions". For, pre-sumably, we *can* so describe a satisfaction which is contingent on the availability of scarce means as distinct from a satisfaction which depends entirely on subjective factors—*e.g.*, the satisfaction of having a summer holiday, as compared with the satisfac-tion of remembering it. But since, as we have seen, the scarcity of means is so wide as to influence in some degree almost all kinds of conduct, this does not seem a useful conception. And since it is mani-festly out of harmony with the main implications of our definition, it is probably best avoided altogether.

It follows, further, that the belief, prevalent among certain critics of Economic Science, that the pre-occupation of the economist is with a peculiarly low type of conduct, depends upon misapprehension. The economist is not concerned with ends as such. He is concerned with the way in which the attainment of ends is limited. The ends may be noble or they may be base. They may be "material" or "immaterial" —if ends can be so described. But if the attainment of one set of ends involves the sacrifice of others, then it has an economic aspect.

All this is quite obvious if only we consider the actual sphere of application of economic analysis, instead of resting content with the assertions of those who do not know what economic analysis is. Suppose, for instance, a community of sybarites, their pleasures

gross and sensual, their intellectual activities pre-
occupied with the "purely material". It is clear
enough that economic analysis can provide categories
for describing the relationships between these ends and
the means which are available for achieving them.
But it is not true, as Ruskin and Carlyle and suchlike
critics have asserted, that it is *limited* to this sort of
thing. Let us suppose this reprehensible community
to be visited by a Savonarola. Their former ends
become revolting to them. The pleasures of the senses
are banished. The sybarites become ascetics. Surely
economic analysis is still applicable. There is no need
to change the categories of explanation. All that has
happened is that the demand schedules have changed.
Some things have become relatively less scarce,
others more so. The rent of vineyards falls. The rent
of quarries for ecclesiastical masonry rises. That is all.
The distribution of time between prayer and good
works has its economic aspect equally with the distribution of time between orgies and slumber. The
"pig-philosophy" — to use Carlyle's contemptuous
epithet—turns out to be all-embracing.

To be perfectly fair, it must be admitted that this is
a case in which economists are to some extent to blame
for their own misfortunes. As we have seen already,
their practice has been more or less unexceptionable.
But their definitions have been misleading, and their
attitude in the face of criticism has been unnecessarily
apologetic. It is even said that quite modern economists who have been convinced both of the importance of Economics *and* of its preoccupation with the
"more material side of human welfare" have been
reduced to prefacing their lectures on general Economic
Theory with the rather sheepish apology that, after

all, bread and butter are necessary, even to the lives of artists and saints. This seems to be unnecessary in itself, and at the same time liable to give rise to misconception in the minds of those who are apt to find the merely material rather small beer. Nevertheless, if Carlyle and Ruskin had been willing to make the intellectual effort necessary to assimilate the body of analysis bequeathed by the great men whom they criticised so unjustly, they would have realised its profound significance in regard to the interpretation of conduct in general, even if they had been unable to provide any better description than its authors. But, as is abundantly clear from their criticisms, they never made this effort. They did not want to make the effort. It was so much easier, so much more congenial, misrepresenting those who did. And the opportunities for misrepresenting a science that had hardly begun to become conscious of its ultimate implications were not far to seek.

But, if there is no longer any excuse for the detractors of Economics to accuse it of preoccupation with particularly low ends of conduct, there is equally no excuse for economists to adopt an attitude of superiority as regards the subjects that they are capable of handling. We have already noticed Professor Cannan's rather paradoxical attitude to a political economy of war. And, speaking generally, are we not entitled to urge that in this respect Professor Cannan is a little apt to follow St. Peter and cry, "Not so, Lord: for nothing common or unclean hath at any time entered into my mouth"? In the opening chapter of *Wealth*,[1] he goes out of his way to say that "the criterion of buying and selling brings

[1] First edition. p. 15.

many things into economics which are not commonly treated there and which it does not seem convenient to treat there. A large trade has existed since history began in supplying certain satisfactions of a sensual character which are never regarded as economic goods. Indulgences to commit what would otherwise be regarded as offences against religion or morality have been sold sometimes openly and at all times under some thin disguise: nobody has regarded these as economic goods". This is surely very questionable. Economists, equally with other human beings, may regard the services of prostitutes as conducive to no "good" in the ultimate ethical sense. But to deny that such services are scarce in the sense in which we use the term, and that there is therefore an economic aspect of hired love, susceptible to treatment in the same categories of general analysis as enable us to explain fluctuations in the price of hired rhetoric, does not seem to be in accordance with the facts. As for the sale of indulgences, surely the status in Economic History of these agreeable transactions is not seriously open to question. Did the sale of indulgences affect the distribution of income, the magnitude of expenditure on other commodities, the direction of production, or did it not? We must not evade the consequences of the conclusion that all conduct coming under the influence of scarcity has its economic aspect.

3. A very interesting example of the difficulties which may arise if the implications which we have been trying to drag into the light are neglected, is afforded in a paper by Sir Josiah Stamp on *Æsthetics as an Economic Factor*.[1] Sir Josiah, in common with

---

[1] *Some Economic Factors in Modern Life*, pp. 1-25.

most men of vision and imagination, is anxious to preserve the countryside and to safeguard ancient monuments. (The occasion of the paper was a decision on the part of his railway company not to destroy Stratford House, a sixteenth-century half-timbered building in Birmingham, to make room for railway sidings.) At the same time, he believes that Economics is concerned with material welfare.[1] He is, therefore, driven to argue that "indifference to the æsthetic will in the long run lessen the economic product; that attention to the æsthetic will increase economic welfare".[2] That is to say, that if we seek first the Kingdom of the Beautiful, all material welfare will be added unto us. And he brings all the solid weight of his authority to the task of stampeding the business world into believing that this is true.

It is easy to sympathise with the intention of the argument. But it is difficult to believe that its logic is very convincing. It may be perfectly true, as Sir Josiah contends, that the wide interests fostered by the study of ancient monuments and the contemplation of beautiful objects are both stimulating to the intelligence and restful to the nervous system, and that, to that extent, a community which offers opportunities for such interests may gain in other, "more material", ways. But it is surely an optimism, unjustified either by experience or by *a priori* probability, to assume that this *necessarily* follows. It is surely a fact which we must all recognise that rejection of material comfort in favour of æsthetic or ethical values does not necessarily bring material compensa-

---

[1] "... I use ... economics as a term to cover the getting of material welfare" (*op. cit.*, p. 3).   [2] *Ibid.*, p. 4.

tion. There are cases when it is *either* bread *or* a lily. Choice of the one involves sacrifice of the other, and, although we may be satisfied with our choice, we cannot delude ourselves that it was not really a choice at all, that more bread will follow. It is not true that all things work together for *material* good to them that love God. So far from postulating a harmony of ends in this sense, Economics brings into full view that conflict of choice which is one of the permanent characteristics of human existence. Your economist is a true tragedian.

What has happened, of course. is that adherence to the "materialist" definition has prevented Sir Josiah from recognising clearly that Economics and Æsthetics are not *in pari materia*.[1] Æsthetics is concerned with certain kinds of ends. The beautiful is an end which offers itself for choice in competition, so to speak, with others. Economics is not concerned at all with any ends *as such*. It is concerned with ends in so far as they affect the disposition of means. It takes the ends as given in scales of relative valuation, and enquires what consequences follow in regard to certain aspects of behaviour.

But, it may be argued, is it not possible to regard the procuring of money as something which competes with other ends, and, if this is so, may we not legitimately speak of an "economic" end of conduct? This raises questions of very great import. Full discussion of the part played in economic analysis of the assumption that money-making is the sole motive of conduct must be deferred until a later chapter, where it will be investigated fully. But, for the

---

[1] It is only fair to state that there are passages in the same essay which seem to be dictated by this sort of consideration, especially the remarks on pp. 14-16 on balance in consumption.

moment, it may be replied that the objection rests
upon a misconception of the significance of money.
Money-making in the normal sense of the term is
merely the intermediate stage between a sale and a
purchase. The procuring of a flow of money from the
sale of one's services or the hiring out of one's property
is not an end *per se*. The money is clearly a means to
ultimate purchase. It is sought, not for itself, but for
the things on which it may be spent—whether these
be the constituents of real income now or of real
income in the future. Money-making in this sense
means securing the means for the achievement of *all*
those ends which are capable of achievement by the
aid of purchasable commodities. Money *as such* is
obviously merely a means—a medium of exchange,
an instrument of calculation. For society, from the
static point of view, the presence of more or less money
is irrelevant. For the individual it is relevant only
in so far as it serves his ultimate objectives. Only the
miser, the psychological monstrosity, desires an infinite accumulation of money. Indeed, so little do we
regard this as typical that, far from regarding the
demand for money to hold as being indefinitely great,
we are in the habit of assuming that money is desired
only to be passed on. Instead of assuming the demand
curve for money to hold to be a straight line parallel
with the y axis, economists have been in the habit
of assuming, as a first approximation, that it is of the
nature of a rectangular hyperbola.[1]

[1] On all this, see Wicksteed, *The Commonsense of Political Economy*,
pp. 155-157. It is not denied that the acquisition of the power to procure
real income may itself become an objective, or that, if it does, the economic
system will not be affected in various ways. All that is contended is that
to label any of these ends "economic" implies a false view of what is necessarily embraced by economic analysis. Economics takes all ends for granted.
They "show" themselves in the scales of relative valuation which are
assumed by the propositions of modern economic analysis.

4. Economics, then, is in no way to be conceived, as we may conceive Ethics or Æsthetics, as being concerned with ends as such. It is equally important that its preoccupations should be sharply distinguished from those of the technical arts of production —with ways of using given means. This raises certain issues of considerable complexity which it is desirable to examine at some length.

The relation between Economics and the technical arts of production is one which has always presented great difficulties to those economists who have thought that they were concerned with the causes of material welfare. It is clear that the technical arts of production are concerned with material welfare. Yet the distinction between art and science does not seem to exhaust the difference. So much scientific knowledge is germane to the technical arts of production that is foreign to Economic Science. Yet where is one to draw the line? Sir William Beveridge has put this difficulty very clearly in his lecture on *Economics as a Liberal Education*. "It is too wide a definition to speak of Economics as the science of the material side of human welfare. A house contributes to human welfare and should be material. If, however, one is considering the building of a house, the question whether the roof should be made of paper or of some other material is a question not of Economics but of the technique of house building".[1] Nor do we meet this difficulty by inserting the word "general" before "causes of material welfare". Economics is not the aggregate of the technologies. Nor is it an attempt to

[1] *Economica*, vol. i., p. 3. Of course the question whether the roof shall be of slate or tiles, for instance, may well depend on the relative prices of these materials and therefore have an economic aspect. Technique merely prescribes certain limits within which choice may operate. See below, p. 35.

select from each the elements common to several. Motion study, for instance, may yield generalisations applicable to more than one occupation. But motion study has nothing to do with Economics. Nor, in spite of the hopes of certain industrial psychologists, is it capable of taking its place. So long as we remain within the ambit of any definition of the subject-matter of Economics in terms of the causes of material welfare, the connection between Economics and the technical arts of production must remain hopelessly obscure.

But, from the point of view of the definition we have adopted, the connection is perfectly definite. The technical arts of production are simply to be grouped among the *given* factors influencing the relative scarcity of different economic goods.[1] The technique of cotton manufacture, as such, is no part of the subject-matter of Economics, but the existence of a given technique of various potentialities, together with the other factors influencing supply, conditions the possible response to any valuation of cotton goods, and consequently influences the adaptations which it is the business of Economics to study.

So far, matters are supremely simple. But now it is necessary to remove certain possible misunderstandings. At first sight it might appear as if the conception we are adopting ran the danger of tipping the baby out with the bath water. In regarding technique as merely data, are we not in danger of

[1] Professor Knight in a recent article ("Economic Science in Recent Discussion", *American Economic Review*, vol. xxiv., p. 225 *et seq.*) complains that I do not make clear that technique in relation to economics is simply so much *data*. I cannot help thinking that the passage above must have escaped Professor Knight's attention. I certainly agree with his views in this respect. But I do not know how to put the matter more strongly than I have done already.

excluding from the subject-matter of Economics just those matters where economic analysis is most at home? For is not production a matter of technique? And is not the theory of production one of the central preoccupations of economic analysis?

The objection sounds plausible. But, in fact, it involves a complete misapprehension—a misapprehension which it is important finally to dispel. The attitude we have adopted towards the technical arts of production does not eliminate the desirability of an economic theory of production.[1] For the influences determining the structure of production are not purely technical in nature. No doubt, technique is very important. But technique is not everything. It is one of the merits of modern analysis that it enables us to put technique in its proper place. This deserves further elucidation. It is not an exaggeration to say that, at the present day, one of the main dangers to civilisation arises from the inability of minds trained in the natural sciences to perceive the difference between the economic and the technical.

Let us consider the behaviour of an isolated man in disposing of a single scarce commodity.[2] Let us consider, for instance, the behaviour of a Robinson Crusoe in regard to a stock of wood of strictly limited dimensions. Robinson has not sufficient wood for all the purposes to which he could put it. For the time being the stock is irreplaceable. What are the influences which will determine the way in which he utilises it?

---

[1] Whether this theory is to be conceived, as it sometimes has been in the past, as concerned with aggregates of wealth is another matter which will be dealt with in the next chapter. See below, Chapter III., Section 6.

[2] Compare Oswalt, *Vorträge über wirtschaftliche Grundbegriffe*, pp. 20-41.

Now, if the wood can only be used at one time and for one purpose, or if it is only wanted at one time and for one purpose, and if we assume that Robinson has ample time to devote to its utilisation, it is perfectly true that his economising will be dictated entirely by his knowledge of the technical arts of production concerned. If he only wants the wood to make a fire of given dimensions, then, if there is only a limited supply of wood available, his activities will be determined by his knowledge of the technique of fire-making. His activities in this respect are purely technical.

But if he wants the wood for more than one purpose—if, in addition to wanting it for a fire, he needs it for fencing the ground round the cabin and keeping the fence in good condition—then, inevitably, he is confronted by a new problem—*the problem of how much wood to use for fires and how much for fencing.* In these circumstances the techniques of fire-making and fencing are still important. But the problem is no longer a purely technical problem.[1] Or, to put the matter another way, the considerations determining his disposal of wood are no longer purely technical. Conduct is the resultant of conflicting psychological pulls acting within an environment of given material and technical possibilities. The problem of technique and the problem of economy are fundamentally different problems. To use Professor Mayer's very elegant way of putting the distinction, the problem of technique arises when there is one end and a multiplicity of means, the problem of economy when both the ends and the means are multiple.[2]

---

[1] All this can be made very clear by the use of a few Paretean curves. Given the production opportunity curves, we know the technical possibilities. But the problem is not determinate unless the consumption indifference curves are also known.　　[2] See Hans Mayer, *op. cit.*, pp. 5 and 6.

Now, as we have seen already, it is one of the characteristics of the world as we find it that our ends are various and that most of the scarce means at our disposal are capable of alternative application. This applies not only to scarce products. It applies still more to the ultimate factors of production. The various kinds of natural resources and labour can be used for an almost infinite variety of purposes. The disposition to abstain from consumption in the present releases uses of primary factors for more than one kind of roundabout process. And, for this reason, a mere knowledge of existing technique does not enable us to determine the actual "set" of the productive apparatus. We need to know also the ultimate valuations of the producers and consumers connected with it. It is out of the interplay of the given systems of ends on the one side and the material and technical potentialities on the other, that the aspects of behaviour which the economist studies are determined. Only in a world in which all goods were free goods would technical considerations be the sole determinants of the satisfaction of given ends. But, in such a world, by definition, the economic problem would have ceased to exist.

All this sounds very abstract. But, in fact, it merely states, in terms of a degree of generality appropriate to the very fundamental questions we are examining, facts which are well known to all of us. If we ask the concrete question, why is the production of such a commodity in such and such an area what it is, and not something else, our answer is not couched in terms which, in the first instance, have a technical implication. Our answer runs in terms of prices and costs; and, as every first-year student knows, prices

and costs are the reflection of relative valuations, not
of merely technical conditions. We all know of commodities which, from the technical point of view,
could be produced quite easily.[1] Yet their production
is not at the moment a business proposition. Why is
this? Because, given the probable price, the costs
involved are too great. And why are costs too great?
Because the technique is not sufficiently developed?
This is only true in a historical sense. But it does
not answer the fundamental question why, *given the
technique*, the costs are too high. And the answer to
that can only be couched in economic terms. It
depends essentially on the price which it is necessary
to pay for the factors of production involved compared with the probable price of the product. And
that may depend on a variety of considerations. In
competitive conditions, it will depend on the valuations placed by consumers on the commodities which
the factors are capable of producing. And if the
costs are too high, that means that the factors of
production can be employed elsewhere producing
commodities which are valued more highly. If the
supply of any factor is monopolised, then high costs
may merely mean that the controllers of the monopoly
are pursuing a policy which leads to some of the factors
they control being temporarily unemployed. But, in
any case, the process of ultimate explanation begins
just where the description of the technical conditions
leaves off.

But this brings us back—although with new knowledge of its implications—to the proposition from
which we started. Economists are not interested in

[1] The production of motor oils from coal is a very topical case in
point.

technique as such. They are interested in it solely as
one of the influences determining relative scarcity.
Conditions of technique "show" themselves in the
productivity functions just as conditions of taste
"show" themselves in the scales of relative valuations. But there the connection ceases. Economics
is a study of the disposal of scarce commodities. The
technical arts of production study the "intrinsic"
properties of objects or human beings.

5. It follows from the argument of the preceding
sections that the subject-matter of Economics is
essentially a series of relationships — relationships
between ends conceived as the possible objectives of
conduct, on the one hand, and the technical and social
environment on the other. Ends as such do not form
part of this subject-matter. Nor does the technical and
social environment. It is the relationships between
these things and not the things in themselves which
are important for the economist.

If this point of view be accepted, a far-reaching
elucidation of the nature of Economic History and
what is sometimes called Descriptive Economics is
possible—an elucidation which renders clear the
relationship between these branches of study and
theoretical Economics and removes all possible
grounds of conflict between them. The nature of
Economic Theory is clear. It is the study of the
formal implications of these relationships of ends and
means on various assumptions concerning the nature
of the ultimate data. The nature of Economic History
should be no less evident. It is the study of the substantial instances in which these relationships show
themselves through time. It is the explanation of
the historical manifestations of "scarcity" Economic

Theory describes the forms, Economic History the substance.

Thus, in regard to Economic History no more than in regard to Economic Theory can we classify events into groups and say: these are the subject-matter of your branch of knowledge and these are not. The province of Economic History, equally with the province of Economic Theory, cannot be restricted to any part of the stream of events without doing violence to its inner intentions. But no more than any other kind of history does it attempt comprehensive description of this stream of events;[1] it concentrates upon the description of a certain *aspect* thereof—a changing network of economic relationships,[2] the effect on values in the economic sense of changes in ends and changes in the technical and social opportunities of realising them.[3] If the Economic Theorist, manipulating his shadowy abacus of forms and inevitable relationships, may comfort himself with the reflection that all action may come under its categories, the Economic Historian, freed from subservience to other branches of history, may rest assured that there is no segment of the multicoloured weft of events which may not prove relevant to his investigations.

[1] On the impossibility of history of any kind without selective principle see Rickert, *Kulturwissenschaft und Naturwissenschaft*, pp. 28-60.

[2] Cp. Cunningham: "Economic History is not so much the study of a special class of facts as the study of all the facts from a special point of view" (*Growth of English Industry and Commerce*, vol. i., p. 8).

[3] On the relation between Economic Theory and Economic History, see Heckscher, *A Plea for Theory in Economic History* (*Economic History*, vol. i., pp. 525-535); Clapham, *The Study of Economic History, passim*; Mises, *Soziologie und Geschichte* (*Archiv für Sozialwissenschaft und Sozialpolitik*, Bd. 61, pp. 465-512). It may be urged that the above description of the nature of Economic History presents a very idealised picture of what is to be found in the average work on Economic History. And it may be admitted that, in the past, Economic History, equally with Economic Theory,

A few illustrations should make this clear. Let us take, for example, that vast upheaval which, for the sake of compendious description, we call the Reformation. From the point of view of the historian of religion, the Reformation is significant in its influence on doctrine and ecclesiastical organisation. From the point of view of the political historian, its interest consists in the changes in political organisation, the new relations of rulers and subjects, the emergence of the national states, to which it gave rise. To the historian of culture it signifies important changes both in the form and the subject-matter of the arts, and the freeing of the spirit of modern scientific enquiry. But to the economic historian it signifies chiefly changes in the distribution of property, changes in the channels of trade, changes in the demand for fish, changes in the supply of indulgences, changes in the incidence of taxes. The economic historian is not interested in the changes of ends and the changes of means in themselves. He is interested only in so far as they affect the series of relationships between means and ends which it is his function to study.

Again, we may take a change in the technical processes of production—the invention of the steam

---

has not always succeeded in purging itself of adventitious elements. In particular it is clear that the influence of the German Historical School was responsible for the intrusion of all sorts of sociological and ethical elements which cannot, by the widest extension of the meaning of words, be described as *Economic* History. It is true too that there has been considerable confusion between Economic History and the economic interpretation of other aspects of history—in the sense of the word "economic" suggested above —and between Economic History and the "Economic Interpretation" of History in the sense of the Materialist Interpretation of History (see below, Section 6). But I venture to suggest the main stream of Economic History from Fleetwood and Adam Smith down to Professor Clapham bears the interpretation put on it here more consistently than any other.

engine or the discovery of rail transport. Events of this sort, equally with changes in ends, have an almost inexhaustible variety of aspects. They are significant for the history of technique, for the history of manners, for the history of the arts, and so on *ad infinitum*. But, for the economic historian, all these aspects are irrelevant save in so far as they involve action and reaction in his sphere of interest. The precise shape of the early steam engine and the physical principles upon which it rested are no concern of the economic historian as economic historian—although economic historians in the past have sometimes displayed a quite inordinate interest in such matters. For him it is significant because it affected the supply of and the demand for certain products and certain factors of production, because it affected the price and income structures of the communities where it was adopted.

So, too, in the field of "Descriptive Economics"— the Economic History of the present day—the main object is always the elucidation of particular "scarcity relationships"—although the attainment of this object often necessarily involves very specialised investigations. In the study of monetary phenomena, for instance, we are often compelled to embark upon enquiries of a highly technical or legal character— the mode of granting overdrafts, the law relating to the issue of paper money. For the banker or the lawyer these things are the focus of attention. But for the economist, although an exact knowledge of them may be essential to his purpose, the acquisition of this knowledge is essentially subservient to his main purpose of explaining the potentialities, in particular situations, of changes in the supply of circulating media. The technical and the legal are of interest solely in so far as they have this aspect.[1]

6. Finally, we may notice the bearing of all this on the celebrated Materialist or "Economic" Interpretation of History. For, from the point of view we have adopted, certain distinctions, not always clearly recognised, are discernible.

We have seen already that, although in the past Economics has been given what may be described as a "materialist" definition, yet its content is not at all materialistic. The change of definition which we have suggested, so far from necessitating a change of content, serves only to make the present content more

[1] Considerations of this sort suggest the very real dangers of overmuch sectionalism in economic studies. In recent years there has been an immense extension of sectional studies in the economic field. We have institutes of Agricultural Economics, Transport Economics, Mining Economics, and so on. And, no doubt, up to a point this is all to the good. In the realm of Applied Economics, some division of labour is essential, and, as we shall see later, theory cannot be fruitfully applied to the interpretation of concrete situations unless it is informed continually of the changing background of the facts of particular industries. But, as experience shows, sectional investigations conducted in isolation are exposed to very grave dangers. If continual vigilance is not exercised they tend to the gradual replacement of economic by technological interests. The focus of attention becomes shifted, and a body of generalisations which have only technical significance comes to masquerade as Economics. And this is fatal. For, since the scarcity of means is relative to *all* ends, it follows that an adequate view of the influences governing social relationships in their economic aspects can only be obtained by viewing the economic system as a whole. In the economic system, "industries" do not live to themselves. Their *raison d'être*, indeed, is the existence of other industries, and their fortunes can only be understood in relation to the whole network of economic relationships. It follows, therefore, that studies which are exclusively devoted to one industry or occupation are continually exposed to the danger of losing touch with the essentials. Their attention may be supposed to be directed to the study of prices and costs, but they tend continually to degenerate either into mere accountancy or into amateur technology. The existence of this danger is no ground for dispensing with this kind of investigation. But it is fundamental that its existence should be clearly recognised. Here as elsewhere, it is the preservation of a proper balance which is important. Our knowledge would be very much poorer if it were not for the existence of many of the various specialised research institutes. But many serious misunderstandings would be avoided if the workers engaged therein would keep more clearly in mind a conception of what is economically relevant.

comprehensible. The "materialism" of Economics was a pseudo-materialism. In fact, it was not materialistic at all.

It might be thought that a similar state of affairs prevailed in regard to the "Economic" or Materialist Interpretation of History—that a mere change of label would suffice to make this doctrine consistent with the modern conception of economic analysis. But this is not so. For the so-called "Economic" Interpretation of History is not only *labelled* "Materialist", it is *in substance* through and through materialistic. It holds that all the events of history, or at any rate all the major events in history, are attributable to "material" changes, not in the philosophical sense that these events are part of the material world, nor in the psychological sense that psychic dispositions are the mere epiphenomena of physiological changes— though, of course, Marx would have accepted these positions—but in the sense that the material technique of production conditions the form of all social institutions, and *all* changes in social institutions are the result of changes in the technique of production. History is the epiphenomenon of technical change. The history of tools is the history of mankind.[1]

Now, whether this doctrine is right or wrong, it is certainly materialistic, and it is certainly not deriva-

---

[1] In what follows, the distinctions I employ are very similar to those used by Dr. Strigl (*op. cit.*, pp. 158-161). The differences in our emphasis may be attributed to a difference of expository purpose. Dr. Strigl is trying to exhibit the Materialist Interpretation as a primitive theory of what he calls *Datenänderung*. He, therefore, tends to slur its deficiency in refusing to take account of changes in ultimate valuations save as derivative from changes on the supply side. I am anxious to show the fundamental distinction between any explanation of history springing from economic analysis as we know it and the explanation attempted by the Materialist Interpretation. I therefore drag this particular point into the light. I do not think that Dr. Strigl would question the logic of my distinctions any more than I would question the interest of his analogy.

tive from Economic Science as we know it. It asserts quite definitely, not only that technical changes cause changes in scarcity relationships and social institutions generally—which would be a proposition in harmony with modern economic analysis—but also that all changes in social relations are due to technical changes—which is a sociological proposition quite outside the limited range of economic generalisation. It definitely implies that all changes in ends, in relative valuations, are conditioned by changes in the technical potentialities of production. It implies, that is to say, that ultimate valuations are merely the by-product of technical conditions. If technical conditions alter, tastes, etc., alter. If they remain unchanged, then tastes, etc., are unaltered. There are no *autonomous* changes on the demand side. What changes occur are, in the end, attributable to changes in the technical machinery of supply. There is no independent "psychological" (or, for that matter, "physiological") side to scarcity. No matter what their fundamental make-up, be it inherited or acquired, men in similar technical environments will develop similar habits and institutions. This may be right or wrong, pseudo-Hegelian twaddle or profound insight into things which at the moment are certainly not susceptible of scientific analysis, but it is not to be deduced from any laws of theoretical Economics. It is a general statement about the causation of human motive which, from the point of view of Economic Science, is completely gratuitous. The label "Materialist" fits the doctrine. The label "Economic" is misplaced. Economics may well provide an important instrument for the elucidation of history. But there is nothing in economic analysis which entitles us to assert that

all history is to be explained in "economic" terms,
if "economic" is to be used as equivalent to the
technically material. The Materialist Interpretation
of History has come to be called the Economic Interpretation of History, because it was thought that the
subject-matter of Economics was "the causes of
material welfare". Once it is realised that this is not
the case, the Materialist Interpretation must stand
or fall by itself. Economic Science lends no support to
its doctrines. Nor does it assume at any point the
connections it asserts. From the point of view of
Economic Science, changes in relative valuations are
data.[1]

[1] It might be argued, indeed, that a thorough understanding of economic
analysis was conducive to presumptions against the Materialist Interpretation. Once it is realised how changes in technique do *directly* influence
amounts demanded, it is extraordinarily difficult to bring oneself to postulate
any *necessary* connection between technical changes and autonomous
changes on the demand side. Such an attitude of scepticism towards the
Marxian theory does not imply denial of metaphysical materialism—
though equally it does not imply its acceptance—it implies merely a refusal
to believe that the causes influencing taste and so on are technical in nature.
The most intransigent behaviourist need find nothing to quarrel with in the
belief that technical materialism in this sense is a very misleading half truth.

CHAPTER III

THE RELATIVITY OF ECONOMIC "QUANTITIES"

1. THAT aspect of behaviour which is the subject-matter of Economics is, as we have seen, conditioned by the scarcity of *given* means for the attainment of *given* ends. It is clear, therefore, that the quality of scarcity in goods is not an "absolute" quality. Scarcity does not mean mere infrequency of occurrence. It means limitation in relation to demand. Good eggs are scarce because, having regard to the demand for them, there are not enough to go round. But bad eggs, of which, let us hope, there are far fewer in existence, are not scarce at all in our sense. They are redundant. This conception of scarcity has implications both for theory and for practice which it is the object of this chapter to elucidate.

2. It follows from what has just been said that the conception of an economic good is necessarily purely formal.[1] There is no quality in things taken out of their relation to men which can make them economic goods. There is no quality in services taken

---

[1] Of course, the conceptions of any pure science are *necessarily* purely formal. If we were attempting to describe Economics by inference from general methodological principles, instead of describing it as it appears from a consideration of what is essential in its subject-matter, this would be a guiding consideration. But it is interesting to observe how, starting from the inspection of an apparatus which actually exists for solving concrete problems, we eventually arrive, by the necessities of accurate description, at conceptions which are in full conformity with the expectations of pure methodology.

out of relation to the end served which makes them economic. Whether a particular thing or a particular service is an economic good depends entirely on its relation to valuations.

Thus wealth[1] is not wealth because of its substantial qualities. It is wealth because it is scarce. We cannot define wealth in physical terms as we can define food in terms of vitamin content or calorific value. It is an essentially relative concept. For the community of ascetics discussed in the last chapter there may be so many goods of certain kinds in relation to the demand for them that they are free goods— not wealth at all in the strict sense. In similar circumstances, the community of sybarites might be "poor". That is to say, for them, the self-same goods might be economic goods.

So, too, when we think of productive power in the economic sense, we do not mean something absolute —something capable of physical computation. We mean power to satisfy given demands. If the given demands change, then productive power in this sense changes also.

A very vivid example of what this means is to be found in Mr. Winston Churchill's account of the situation confronting the Ministry of Munitions at 11 a.m. on November 11th, 1918—the moment of the signing of the Armistice. After years of effort, the nation had acquired a machine for turning out the

---

[1] The term wealth is used here as equivalent to a flow of economic goods. But I think it is clear that there are profound disadvantages in using it in this sense. It would be very paradoxical to have to maintain that, if "economic" goods by reason of multiplication became "free" goods, wealth would diminish. Yet that might be urged to the implication of this usage. Hence, in any rigid delimitation of Economics, the term wealth should be avoided. It is used here simply in elucidation of the implications for everyday discussion of the somewhat remote propositions of the preceding paragraph.

materials of war in unprecedented quantities. Enormous programmes of production were in every stage of completion. Suddenly the whole position is changed. The "demand" collapses. The needs of war are at an end. What was to be done? Mr. Churchill relates how, in the interests of a smooth change-over, instructions were issued that material more than 60 per cent. advanced was to be finished. "Thus for many weeks after the war was over we continued to disgorge upon the gaping world masses of artillery and military materials of every kind."[1] "It was waste", he adds, "but perhaps it was a prudent waste." Whether this last contention is correct or not is irrelevant to the point under discussion. What is relevant is that what at 10.55 a.m. that morning was wealth and productive power, at 11.5 had become "not-wealth," an embarrassment, a source of social waste. The substance had not changed. The guns were the same. The potentialities of the machines were the same. From the point of view of the technician, everything was exactly the same. But from the point of view of the economist, everything was different. Guns, explosives, lathes, retorts, all had suffered a sea change. The ends had changed. The scarcity of means was different.[2]

---

[1] *The World Crisis*, vol. v., pp. 33-35.

[2] It is, perhaps, worth while observing how our practice here differs from the practice which would seem to follow from Professor Cannan's procedure. Having defined wealth as material welfare, Professor Cannan would be logically compelled to argue that we were not producing during the War. In fact, he gets out of the difficulty by arguing that we may say that we were producing produce but not material welfare (*Review of Economic Theory*, p. 51). From the point of view of the definitions here adopted, it follows, not that we were not producing, but simply that we were not producing for the same demands as during peace time. From either point of view, the *non-comparability* of material statistics of war and peace follows clearly. But from our point of view the *persistence* of formal economic laws is much more clearly emphasised.

3. The proposition which we have just been discussing, concerning what may be described as the relativity of "economic quantities", has an important bearing on many problems of Applied Economics—so important, indeed, that it is worth while, here and now, interrupting the course of our main argument in order to examine them rather more fully. There can be no better illustration of the way in which the propositions of pure theory facilitate comprehension of the meaning of concrete issues.

A conspicuous instance of a type of problem which can only be satisfactorily solved with the aid of the distinctions we have been developing, is to be found in contemporary discussions of the alleged economies of mass production. At the present day the lay mind is dominated by the spectacular achievements of mass production. Mass production has become a sort of cure-all, an open sesame. The goggled eyes of the world turn westward to Ford the deliverer. He who has gaped longest at the conveyors at Detroit is hailed as the most competent economist.

Now, naturally, no economist in his senses would wish to deny the importance for modern civilisation of the potentialities of modern manufacturing technique. The technical changes which bring to the door, even of the comparatively poor man, the motor-car, the gramophone, the wireless apparatus, are truly momentous changes. But, in judging their significance in regard to a given set of ends, it is very important to bear in mind this distinction between the mere multiplication of material objects and the satisfaction of demand, which the definitions of this chapter elucidate. To use a convenient jargon, it is important to bear in mind the distinction between technical and

4

value productivity. The mass production of particular things irrespective of demand for them, however technically efficient, is not necessarily "economical". As we have seen already, there is a fundamental difference between technical and economic problems.[1] We may take it as obvious that, within certain limits (which, of course, change with changing conditions of technique), specialisation of men and machinery is conducive to technical efficiency. But the extent to which such specialisation is "economical" depends essentially upon the extent of the market—that is to say, upon demand.[2] For a blacksmith producing for a small and isolated community to specialise solely on the production of a certain type of horse-shoe, in order to secure the economies of mass production, would be folly. After he has made a limited number of shoes of one size, it is clearly better for him to turn his attention to producing shoes of other sizes, additional units of which will be more urgently demanded than additional units of the size of which he has already manufactured a large quantity.

So, too, in the world at large at any particular moment, there are definite limits to the extent to which the mass production of any one type of commodity to the exclusion of other types is in conformity with the demands of consumers. If it is carried beyond these limits, not only is there waste, in the sense that productive power is used to produce goods of less value than could be produced otherwise, but there is also definite financial loss for the productive enterprise concerned. It is one of the paradoxes of the history of

[1] See above, pp. 32-38.

[2] See Allyn Young, *Increasing Returns and Economic Progress* (*Economic Journal*, vol. xxxviii., pp. 528-542). On the sense in which it is legitimate to use the term "economical" in this connection, see Chapter VI. below.

modern thought that, at a time when the disproportionate development of particular lines of production
has wrought more chaos in the economic system than
at any earlier period in history, there should arise the
naïve belief that a general resort to mass production,
whenever and wherever it is technically possible,
regardless of the conditions of demand, will see us out
of our difficulties. It is the nemesis of the worship of
the machine, the paralysis of the intellect of a world
of technicians.

This confusion between technical potentiality and
economic value, which, borrowing a phrase of Professor
Whitehead's, we may call the "fallacy of misplaced
concreteness",[1] also underlies certain notions at
present unduly prevalent with regard to the value
of fixed capital. It is sometimes thought that the
fact that large sums of money have been sunk in
certain forms of fixed capital renders it undesirable,
if consumer's demand changes, or if technical invention renders it possible to satisfy a given consumer's
demand in other more profitable ways, that the capital
should fall into disuse. If the satisfaction of demand
is assumed as the criterion of economic organisation,
this belief is completely fallacious. If I purchase a
railway ticket from London to Glasgow, and half-way
on my journey I receive a telegram informing me that
my appointment must take place in Manchester, it
is not rational conduct for me to continue my journey
northwards, just because I have "sunk capital" in
the ticket which I am unable to recover. It is true that
the ticket is still as "technically efficient" in procuring
me the right to go to Glasgow. But my objective has
now changed. The power to continue my journey

---

[1] *Science and the Modern World*, p. 84.

northward is no longer valuable to me. To continue nevertheless would be irrational. In Economics, as Jevons remarked, bygones are forever bygones.

Exactly similar considerations apply when we are considering the present status of machinery for whose products demand has ceased, or which has ceased to be as profitable, taking everything into account, as other kinds of machinery. Although the machinery may be technically as efficient as it was before these changes, yet its economic status is different.[1] No doubt, *if* the change in demand or in cost conditions which led to its supersession had been foreseen, the disposition of resources would have been different. In that sense it is not meaningless to speak of a waste due to ignorance—although there are difficulties here. But once the change has taken place, what has happened before is totally irrelevant—it is waste to take it into further consideration. The problem is one of adjustment to the situation that is given. When every legitimate criticism of the subjective theory of value has been taken into account, it still remains the unshakable achievement of this theory that it focuses attention on this fact, as important in applied Economics as in the purest of pure theory.

As a last example of the importance for applied Economics of the propositions we have been considering, we may examine certain misconceptions

---

[1] Compare Pigou, *Economics of Welfare*, 3rd edition, pp. 190-192. It is, perhaps, worth noting that most contemporary discussion of the so-called Transport Problem completely ignores these elementary considerations. If there is a concealed subsidy to motor transport through public expenditure on roads, this is a matter for the Chancellor of the Exchequer. It is no argument for attempting to make people go by train who prefer to travel by road. If we want to preserve railways which are unprofitable in the present conditions of demand, we should subsidise them as ancient monuments.

with regard to the economic effects of inflation. It is a well-known fact that during periods of inflation there is often for a time extreme activity in the constructional industries. Under the stimulus of the artificially low interest rates, overhauling of capital equipment on the most extensive scale is often undertaken. New factories are built. Old factories are re-equipped. To the lay mind, there is something extraordinarily fascinating about this spectacular activity; and when the effects of inflation are being discussed, it is not infrequently regarded as a virtue that it should be instrumental in bringing this about. How often does one hear it said of the German inflation that, while it was painful enough while it lasted, it did at least provide German industry with a new capital equipment. Indeed, no less an authority than Professor F. B. Graham has given the weight of his authority to this view.[1]

But, plausible as all this may seem, it is founded on the same crude materialist conception as the other fallacies we have been discussing. For the efficiency of any industrial system does not consist in the presence of large quantities of up-to-date capital equipment, irrespective of the demand for its products or the price of the factors of production which are needed for the profitable exploitation of such equipment. It consists in the degree of adaptation to meet demand of the organisation of *all* resources. Now it

---

[1] *Exchange, Prices and Production in Hyperinflation : Germany*, 1920-1923, p. 320. "So far as output is concerned, there is little support in actual statistics for the contention that the evils of inflation were other than evils of distribution." In his conclusion, Professor Graham does indeed make the grudging admission that "in the later stages of inflation, investment in durable goods took on a bizarre aspect". But he seems to believe that the "quality" of capital equipment may deteriorate without any detriment to its "quantity".

can be shown[1] that, during times of inflation, the artificially low rates of interest tend to encourage expansion of certain kinds of capitalistic production in such measure that, when the stimulus is exhausted, it is no longer possible to work them as profitable undertakings. At the same time, liquid resources are dissipated and exhausted. When the slump comes, the system is left high and dry with an incubus of fixed capital too costly to be worked at a profit, and a relative shortage of "liquid capital" which causes interest rates to be stringent and oppressive. The beautiful machinery which so impressed the newspaper correspondents is still there, but the wheels are empty of profit. The material is there. But it has lost its economic significance. Considerations of this sort might have been thought to be very remote from reality at the time of the German inflation or at the time of stabilisation. After years of chronic "capital shortage" in that unhappy country, they begin to appear less paradoxical.[2]

4. It is time to return to more abstract considerations. We have next to consider the bearing of our definitions upon the meaning of Economic Statistics.

Economic Statistics employ two kinds of units of reckoning—physical units and value units. Reckoning is by "weight and tale" or by valuation—so many tons of coal, so many pounds sterling worth of coal. From the point of view of economic analysis, what meaning is to be attached to these computations?

[1] See Mises, *The Theory of Money and Credit*, pp. 339-366; Hayek, *Monetary Theory and the Trade Cycle*, and *Prices and Production*; Strigl, *Die Produktion unter dem Einflusse einer Kreditexpansion* (*Schriften des Vereins für Sozialpolitik*, Bd. 173, pp. 187-211).

[2] See Bonn, *Das Schicksal des deutschen Kapitalismus*, pp. 14-31. Bresciani-Turroni, *Il Vicendi del Marco Tedesco*.

So far as physical reckonings are concerned, what has been said already is sufficient. There is no need further to labour the proposition that, although, as records of fact, physical computations may be unimpeachable and, in certain connections, useful, yet from the point of view of the economist they have no significance apart from relative valuations. No doubt, assuming a certain empirical permanence of relative valuations, many physical series have direct significance for applied Economics. But from the logical point of view this is an accident. The significance of the series always depends upon the background of relative valuation.

So far as reckonings in terms of value are concerned, there are other subtler difficulties which we must now proceed to unravel.

According to modern price theory, the prices of different commodities and factors of production are expressions of relative scarcity, or, in other words, marginal valuations.[1] Given an initial distribution of resources, each individual entering the market may be conceived to have a scale of relative valuations; and the interplay of the market serves to bring these individual scales and the market scale as expressed in relative prices into harmony with one another.[2] Prices, therefore, express in money a grading of the various goods and services coming on the market. Any given price, therefore, has significance only in relation to the other prices prevailing at that time. Taken by itself it means nothing. It is only as the expression in money terms of a certain order of preference that it means anything at all. As Samuel

---

[1] See below, Chapter IV., Section 2.

[2] For an exhaustive description of the process, see especially Wicksteed, *Commonsense of Political Economy*, pp. 212-400.

Bailey pointed out over a hundred years ago, "As we cannot speak of the distance of any object without implying some other object between which and the former this relation exists, so we cannot speak of the value of a commodity, but in reference to another commodity compared with it. A thing cannot be valuable in itself without reference to another thing, any more than a thing can be distant in itself without reference to another thing."[1]

It follows from this that the term which, for the sake of continuity and to raise certain definite associations, we have used hitherto in this chapter, the term "economic *quantity*" is really very misleading. A price, it is true, expresses the quantity of money which it is necessary to give in exchange for a given commodity. But its significance is the relationship between this quantity of money and other similar quantities. And the valuations which the price system expresses are not quantities at all. They are arrangements in a certain order. To assume that the scale of relative prices measures any quantity at all save quantities of money is quite unnecessary. Value is a relation, not a measurement.[2]

But, if this is so, it follows that the addition of prices or individual incomes to form social aggregates

---

[1] *A Critical Dissertation on Value*, p. 5.

[2] Recognition of the ordinal nature of the valuations implied in price is fundamental. It is difficult to overstress its importance. With one slash of Occam's razor, it extrudes for ever from economic analysis the last vestiges of psychological hedonism. The conception is implicit in Menger's use of the term *Bedeutung* in his statement of the Theory of Value, but the main credit for its explicit statement and subsequent elaboration is due to subsequent writers. See especially Čuhel, *Zur Lehre von den Bedürfnissen*, pp. 186-216; Pareto, *Manuel d'Economie Politique*, pp. 540-2; and Hicks and Allen, *A Reconsideration of the Theory of Value* (*Economica*, 1934, pp. 51-76). In this important article it is shown how the most refined conceptions of the theory of value, complementarity, substitutability, etc., may be developed without recourse to the notion of a determinate utility function.

is an operation with a very limited meaning. As quantities of money expended, particular prices and particular incomes are capable of addition, and the total arrived at has a definite monetary significance. But as expressions of an order of preference, a relative scale, they are incapable of addition. Their aggregate has no meaning. They are only significant in relation to each other. Estimates of the social income may have a quite definite meaning for monetary theory. But beyond this they have only *conventional* significance.

It is important to realise exactly both the weight and the limitations of this conclusion. It does mean that a comprehensive aggregate of prices means nothing but a stream of money payments. Both the concept of world money income and the national money income have strict significance only for monetary theory—the one in relation to the general theory of indirect exchange, the other to the Ricardian theory of the distribution of the precious metals. But, of course, this does not exclude a *conventional* significance. If we like to assume that preferences and distribution do not change rapidly within short periods, and that certain price changes may be regarded as particularly significant for the majority of economic subjects, then no doubt we may assign to the movements of these aggregates a certain arbitrary meaning which is not without its uses. And this is all that is claimed for such estimates by the best statisticians. All that is intended here is to emphasise the essentially arbitrary nature of the assumptions necessary. They do not have an exact counterpart in fact, and they do not follow from the main categories of pure theory.

We can see the bearing of all this if we consider for a moment the use which may be made of such aggregates in examining the probable effects of drastic changes in distribution. From time to time computations are made of the total money income accruing within a given area, and, from these totals, attempts are made to estimate the effects of large changes in an equalitarian direction. The best known of such attempts are the estimates of Professor Bowley and Sir Josiah Stamp.[1]

Now, in so far as such estimates are confined to ascertaining the initial amount of spending power available for redistribution, they are valuable and important. And, of course, this is all that has ever been contended by the distinguished statisticians who put them forward. But beyond this it is futile to attach any precise significance to them. For, by the very fact of redistribution, relative valuations would necessarily alter. The whole "set" of the productive machine would be different. The stream of goods and services would have a different composition. Indeed, if we think a little further into the problem, we can see that an estimate of this sort must very grossly overestimate the amount of productive power that would be released by such changes. For a substantial proportion of the high incomes of the rich are due to the existence of other rich persons. Lawyers, doctors, the proprietors of rare sites, etc., enjoy high incomes because there exist people with high incomes who value their services highly. Redistribute money incomes, and, although the technical efficiency of the factors concerned would be the same, their place on the relative scale would be entirely different. With a constant volume of money and a constant velocity

[1] See Bowley, *The Division of the Product of Industry*, and Stamp, *Wealth and Taxable Capacity*.

of circulation, it is almost certain that the main initial result would be a rise in the prices of articles of working-class consumption. This conclusion, which is obvious enough from the census of occupations, tends actually to be concealed by computations in money—pessimistic as these computations are often supposed to be. If we compute the proportion of the population now producing real income for the rich who could be turned to producing real income for the poor, it is easy to see that the increase available would be negligible. If we attempt greater precision by means of money computations, we are likely to exaggerate. And the greater the degree of initial inequality, the greater the degree of exaggeration.[1]

5. It is a further consequence of the conception of value as an expression of an order of preference that comparisons of prices have no precise significance, unless exchange is possible between the commodities whose prices are being compared.

It follows, therefore, that to compare the prices of a particular commodity at different periods of time in the past, is an operation which, by itself, does not necessarily afford results which have further meaning. The fact that bread last year was 8d. and bread this year is 6d. does not necessarily imply that the relative scarcity of bread this year is less than the relative scarcity of bread last year. The significant comparison

---

[1] Of course, this is not necessarily so. If, instead of spending their incomes on the expensive services of doctors, lawyers, and so on, the rich were in the habit of spending them on vast retinues of retainers *who were supported by the efforts of others*, the change in money incomes might release factors which, from the point of view of the new conditions of demand, represented much productive power. But in fact this is not the case. Even when the rich do support vast retinues of retainers, the retainers spend most of their time looking after each other. Anyone who has lived in a household in which there was more than one servant will realise the force of this consideration.

is not the comparison between 8d. last year and 6d. this year, but the comparison between 8d. and other prices last year and the comparison between 6d. and other prices this year. For it is these relationships which are significant for conduct. It is these relationships alone which imply a unitary system of valuations.[1]

At one time it used to be thought that these difficulties could be overcome by correcting individual prices for variations in the "value of money". And it may be admitted that, if the relations between each commodity and all the others save the one under consideration remained the same, and only the supply of money and the demand or supply of this particular commodity altered, such corrections would be sufficient. If, that is to say, the original price relationships were

$$P_a = P_b = P_c = P_d = P_e \quad . \quad . \quad . \quad . \quad (1)$$

and in the next period they were

$$P_a = \tfrac{1}{2}P_b = \tfrac{1}{2}P_c = \tfrac{1}{2}P_d = \tfrac{1}{2}P_e \quad . \quad . \quad . \quad (2)$$

then matters would be simple, and the comparison would have some meaning. But such a relationship is

---

[1] On all this, the classical discussion is still to be found in Samuel Bailey's chapter (*op. cit.*, pp. 71-93) "On comparing commodities at different periods". Bailey overstates his case to this extent, that he does not mention *prospective* value relations through time (see below, p. 61). But in every other respect his position is unassailable, and his demonstrations are among the most elegant to be found in the whole range of theoretical analysis. Even the most *blasé* could scarcely resist a thrill at the exquisite delicacy of his exhibition of the ambiguities of the first proposition of Ricardo's *Principles*. It was one of the few real injuries done to the progress of Economic Science by the solidarity of the English Classics that, presumably because of its attacks on Ricardo and Malthus, Bailey's work was allowed to drop into neglect. It is hardly an exaggeration to say that the theory of index number is only today emancipating itself from errors into which a regard to Bailey's main proposition would effectively have prevented it from falling.

not possible save as a result of a series of compensatory accidents. This is not merely because demand or the conditions of production of *other commodities* may change. It is because almost any conceivable change, either real or monetary, must bring about *different* changes in the relation of a particular good to each other commodity. That is to say, save in the case of a compensatory accident, any change will lead not to a new set of relationships of the order of equation (2), but rather to a set of relationships of the order

$$P_a = \tfrac{1}{2}P_b = \tfrac{1}{4}P_c = \tfrac{3}{4}P_d = P_e \ . \ . \ . \ . \ (3)$$

It has long been recognised that this must be the case with real changes. If the demand for a changes, it is most improbable that the demand for b, c, d, e . . . will change in such a way that the change in relation between a and b will be equivalent to the change in relation to b and c . . . and so on. With changes in technique, factors of production which are released from the production of a will not be likely to be distributed between b, c, d in such proportions as to preserve $P_b : P_c :: P_c : P_d$ . . . But, as may be demonstrated by very elementary reasoning,[1] the same is true of "monetary" changes. It is almost impossible to conceive a "monetary" change which does not affect relative prices differently. But, if this is so, the idea of precise "correction" of price changes over time is illusory.[2] Samuel Bailey's conclusion remains: "When we say that an article in a former

---

[1] See especially Hayek, *Prices and Production*, ch. iii.

[2] It is not always realised that the difficulty of attaching precise meaning to the idea of changes in value, if there are more than two commodities and the ratios of exchange between one and the rest do not move in the same proportion, is not limited to the idea of changes in the "value of money". The problem of conceiving changes in the "purchasing power" of pig iron is just as insoluble as the problem of conceiving changes in the purchasing power of money. The difference is a practical one. The fact that

age was of a certain value, we mean that it exchanged for a certain quantity of some other commodity. But this is an inapplicable expression in speaking of only one commodity at two different periods."[1]

It is important to realise the exact significance of this proposition. It does not deny the possibility of intertemporal price relationships. Quite clearly, at any moment, anticipations of what prices will be at a future period inevitably influence present valuations and price relationships.[2] It is possible to exchange goods now for goods in the future, and we can conceive an equilibrium direction of price change through time. This is true and important. But while there is and must be a connection between present prices and anticipations of future prices, there is no necessary connection or significant value relationship between present prices and *past prices*. The conception of an equilibrium relationship through time is a hypothetical relationship. It is realised only in so far as anticipations are proved to have been justified. Through history, the data change, and though *at every moment* there may be tendencies towards an equilibrium, yet *from moment to moment* it is not the *same* equilibrium towards which there is movement. There is a fundamental asymmetry in price relationships through time. The future—the apparent future, that is to say—affects the present, but the past is irrelevant. The effects of the past are now simply part of the data.

---

production is determined by relative valuations makes it unnecessary for practical purposes to worry about changes in the purchasing power of pig iron, while for all sorts of reasons, some good, some bad, we are obliged to worry a good deal about the effects of "monetary" changes.

[1] *Op. cit.*, p. 72.

[2] See Fetter, *Economic Principles*, p. 101 *ff.*, and pp. 235-277. See also Hayek, *Das intertemporale Gleichgewichtsystem der Preise und die Bewegungen des "Geldwertes"* (*Weltwirtschaftliches Archiv*, Bd. 28, pp. 33-76).

So far as the act of valuation is concerned, bygones are forever bygones.

Here, again, as in the case of our considerations regarding aggregates, there is no intention of denying the practical utility and significance of comparisons of certain prices over time, or of the value of "corrections" of these prices by suitably devised index numbers. It is not open to serious question that for certain questions of applied Economics on the one hand, and interpretation of history on the other, the index number technique is of great practical utility. Given a willingness to make arbitrary assumptions with regard to the significance of certain price sums, it is not denied that conclusions which are important for practice may be reached. All that it is desired to emphasise is that such conclusions do not follow from the categories of pure theory, and that they must necessarily involve a *conventional* element depending either upon the assumption of a certain empirical constancy of data[1] or upon arbitrary judgments of value with regard to the relative importance of particular prices and particular economic subjects.

6. The interpretation of economic statistics is not

[1] As in discussions of changes in real income and the cost of living. On all this see Haberler, *Der Sinn der Indexzahlen, passim.* Dr. Haberler's con clusion is definitive. "Die Wissenschaft macht sich einer Grenzüberschreitung schuldig, sie fällt ein Werturteil wenn sie die Wirtschaftsubjekte belehren will welches von zwei Naturaleinkommen das 'grössere' Realeinkommen enthält. Darüber zu entscheiden, welches vorzuziehen ist, sind einzig und allein die Wirtschafter selbst berufen," p. 83 ("Science is guilty of trespassing beyond its necessary limits—that is to say, it is delivering a judgment of value—if it attempts to lay down for others which of two real incomes is the 'larger'. To decide on this, to decide which real income is to be preferred, is a task which can only be done by him who is to enjoy it— that is, by the individual as 'economic subject'". The translation is very free, for there is no English equivalent to the very useful German contrast between *Naturaleinkommen* and *Realeinkommen* unless we use "Real income" as equivalent to *Naturaleinkommen* and Fetter's "Psychic income" for the German *Realeinkommen*).

the only department of economic studies to be affected by this conception of our subject-matter. The arrangement and elaboration of the central body of theoretical analysis is also considerably modified. This is an interesting example of the utility of this kind of investigation. Starting from the intention to state more precisely the subject of our generalisations, we reach a point of view which enables us, not only to pick out what is essential and what is accidental in those generalisations, but also to restate them in such a way as to give their essential bearing much greater force. Let us see how this happens.

The traditional approach to Economics, at any rate among English-speaking economists, has been by way of an enquiry into the causes determining the production and distribution of wealth.[1] Economics has been divided into two main divisions, the theory of production and the theory of distribution, and the task of these theories has been to explain the causes determining the size of the "total product" and the causes determining the proportions in which it is distributed between different factors of production and different persons. There have been minor differences of content under these two headings. There has always been a great deal of trouble about the position of the theory of value. But, speaking broadly, up to quite a recent date, this has been the main "cut" into the body of the subject.

Now, no doubt, there is a strong *prima facie* case for this procedure. As Professor Cannan urges,[2] the

---

[1] See Cannan, *Theories of Production and Distribution*, ch. ii.

[2] "The fundamental questions of economics are why all of us taken together are as well off as we are and why some of us are much better off and others much worse off than the average . . ." (Cannan, *Wealth*, 3rd edition, p. v).

questions in which we are interested from the point of view of social policy are—or at any rate appear to be —questions relating to production and distribution. If we are contemplating the imposition of a tax or the granting of a subsidy, the questions we tend to ask (whether we understand what we mean or not) are: What will be the effects of this measure on production? What will be its effects on distribution? It is not unnatural, therefore, that, in the past, economists have tended to arrange their generalisations in the form of answers to these two questions.[1]

Yet, if we bear in mind what has been said already with regard to the nature of our subject-matter and the relativity of the "quantities" it contemplates, it should be fairly clear that from this point of view the traditional division has serious deficiencies.

It should not be necessary at this stage to dwell upon the inappropriateness of the various technical elements which almost inevitably intrude into a system arranged on this principle. We have all felt, with Professor Schumpeter, a sense almost of shame at the incredible banalities of much of the so-called theory of production—the tedious discussions of the various forms of peasant proprietorship, factory organisation, industrial psychology, technical education, etc., which are apt to occur in even the best treatises on general theory arranged on this plan.[2]

[1] Whether their generalisations *did* answer the questions, especially that relating to personal distribution, is another matter (see Cannan, *Economic Outlook*, pp. 215-253, and *Review of Economic Theory*, pp. 284-332; see also Dalton, *Inequality of Incomes*, pp. 33-158). The point is that they thought they ought to answer them. The fact that they did not is not necessarily to the discredit either of economists or their generalisations. There is strong reason for supposing that personal distribution is determined in part by extra-economic causes.

[2] See Schumpeter, *Das Wesen und der Hauptinhalt der theoretischen Nationalökonomie*, p. 156.

But there is a more fundamental objection to this procedure; it necessarily precludes precision. Scientific generalisations, if they are to pretend to the status of laws, must be capable of being stated exactly. That does not mean, as we shall see in a later chapter, that they must be capable of quantitative exactitude. We do not need to give numerical values to the law of demand to be in a position to use it for deducing important consequences. But we do need to state it in such a way as to make it relate to formal relations which are capable of being *conceived* exactly.[1]

Now, as we have seen already, the idea of changes in the total volume of production has no precise content. We may, if we please, attach certain conventional values to certain indices and say that we *define* a change in production as a change in this index; for certain purposes this may be advisable. But there is no analytical justification for this procedure. It does not follow from our conception of an economic good. The kind of empirical generalisation which may be made concerning what causes will affect production in this sense, can never achieve the status of a law. For a law must relate to definite conceptions and relationships; and a change in the aggregate of production is not a definite conception.

As a matter of fact, nothing which can really be called a "law" of production in this sense has ever been elaborated.[2] Whenever the generalisations of

[1] See Edgeworth, *Mathematical Psychics*, pp. 1-6; Kaufmann, *Was kann die mathematische Methode in der Nationalökonomie leisten?* (*Zeitschrift für Nationalökonomie*, Bd. 2, pp. 754-779).

[2] The nearest approach to a law of production is embodied in the celebrated Optimum Theory of Population. This starts from the perfectly precise law of Non-proportional Returns which relates to variations of productivity in the proportionate combinations of individual factors, and *appears* to achieve a similar precision in regard to variations of all human

economists have assumed the form of laws, they have related not to vague notions such as the total product, but to perfectly definite concepts such as price, supply, demand, and so on. The Ricardian System which, in this respect, provides the archetype of all subsequent systems, is essentially a discussion of the tendencies to equilibrium of clear-cut quantities and relationships. It is no accident that wherever its discussions have related to separate types of economic goods and ratios of exchange between economic goods, there the generalisations of Economics have assumed the form of scientific laws.[1]

For this reason, in recent years economists have tended more and more to abandon the traditional arrangement. We no longer enquire concerning the causes determining variations of production and distribution. We enquire rather concerning the conditions of equilibrium of various economic "quantities",[2] given certain initial data, and we enquire concerning the effects of variations of these data. Instead of

---

factors in a fixed material environment. In fact, however, it introduces conceptions of averages and aggregates to which it is impossible to give meaning without conventional assumptions. On the Optimum Theory see my *Optimum Theory of Population* in *London Essays in Economics*, edited by Dalton and Gregory. In that essay I discussed the difficulties of averaging, but I had not then perceived the full weight of the general methodological difference between statements relating to averages and statements relating to precise quantities. Hence my emphasis on this point is insufficient.

[1] It is important not to overstress the excellence of past procedure. The theory of money, *e.g.*, although in many respects the most highly developed branch of Economic Theory, has continually employed pseudo-concepts of the sort we have just declared suspect—the price level, movements of purchasing power parities, etc. But it is just here that the difficulties of monetary theory have persisted. And recent improvements in monetary theory have been directed to eliminating all dependence on these fictions.

[2] On the various types of equilibrium contemplated, see Knight, *Risk, Uncertainty and Profit*, p. 143, note; Wicksell, *Lectures on Political Economy*, vol. i; and Robbins, *On a Certain Ambiguity in the Conception of Stationary Equilibrium* (*Economic Journal*, vol. xl., pp. 194-214).

dividing our central body of analysis into a theory of
production and a theory of distribution, we have
a theory of equilibrium, a theory of comparative
statics and a theory of dynamic change. Instead
of regarding the economic system as a gigantic machine for turning out an aggregate product and
proceeding to enquire what causes make this product
greater or less, and in what proportions this product
is divided, we regard it as a series of interdependent
but conceptually discrete relationships between men
and economic goods; and we ask under what conditions these relationships are constant and what are
the effects of changes in either the ends or the means
between which they mediate and how such changes
may be expected to take place through time.[1]

As we have seen already, this tendency, although
in its completest form very modern indeed, has its
origin very early in the literature of scientific Economics. Quesnay's *Tableau Economique* was essentially
an attempt to apply what is now called equilibrium
analysis. And, although Adam Smith's great work
professed to deal with the causes of the wealth of
nations, and did in fact make many remarks on the
general question of the conditions of opulence which
are of great importance in any history of applied
Economics, yet, from the point of view of the history
of theoretical Economics, the central achievement of
his book was his demonstration of the mode in which
the division of labour tended to be kept in equilibrium
by the mechanism of relative prices—a demonstration

---

[1] See Pareto, *Manuel d'Economie Politique*, p. 147 ; also my article on
Production in the *Encyclopædia of the Social Sciences*. In the first edition
of this essay I subsumed the theory of comparative statics and the theory
of dynamic change under the single heading, "Theory of Variations." I now
think it it better to make explicit the two types of variation theory. For further elucidations see below, Chapter IV. Section 7.

which, as Allyn Young has shown,[1] is in harmony with the most refined apparatus of the modern School of Lausanne. The theory of value and distribution was really the central core of the analysis of the Classics, try as they might to conceal their objects under other names. And the traditional theory relating to the effects of taxes and bounties was always couched in terms thoroughly consistent with the procedure of modern comparative statics. Thus, though the appearance of modern theory may be new, its substance is continuous with what was most essential in the old. The modern arrangement simply makes explicit the methodological foundations of the earlier theories and generalises the procedure.[2]

At first sight it might be thought that these innovations ran the risk of over-austerity; that they involved dispensing with a mass of theory which is genuinely illuminating. Such a belief would be founded on an absence of knowledge of the potentialities of the new procedure. It may safely be asserted that there is nothing which fits into the old framework, which cannot be more satisfactorily exhibited in the new. The only difference is that, at every step in the new arrangement, we know exactly the limitations and implications of our knowledge. If we step outside the

[1] *Op cit.*, pp. 540-542.

[2] The beginning of the change dates from the coming of the subjective theory of value. So long as the theory of value was expounded in terms of costs, it was possible to regard the subject-matter of Economics as something social and collective, and to discuss price relationships simply as market phenomena. With the realisation that these market phenomena were, in fact, dependent on the interplay of individual choice, and that the very social phenomena in terms of which they were explained—costs—were in the last analysis the reflex of individual choice—the valuation of alternative opportunities (Wieser, Davenport)—this approach becomes less and less convenient. The work of the mathematical economists in this respect only sets out particularly boldly a procedure which is really common to all modern theory.

sphere of pure analysis and adopt any of the conventional assumptions of applied Economics, we know just where we are. We are never in danger of asserting as an implication of our fundamental premises something which is smuggled in on the way by means of a conventional assumption.

We may take as an example of the advantages of this procedure the modern treatment of organisation of production. The old treatment of this subject was very unsatisfactory: A few trite generalisations about the advantages of the division of labour copied from Adam Smith, and illustrated perhaps by a few examples from Babbage; then extensive discursions on industrial "forms" and the "entrepreneur" with a series of thoroughly unscientific and question-begging remarks on national characteristics—the whole wound up, perhaps, with a chapter on localisation. There is no need to dwell on the dreariness and mediocrity of all this. But it is perhaps just as well to state definitely its considerable positive deficiencies. It suggests that from the point of view of the economist "organisation" is a matter of internal industrial (or agricultural) arrangement—if not internal to the firm, at any rate internal to "the" industry—although, as might be expected, "the" industry is seldom satisfactorily defined. At the same time it tends to leave out completely the governing factor of all productive organisation — the relationship of prices and costs. That comes in a different division which deals with "value". As a result, as almost any teacher who has taken over students reared on the old textbooks will realise, it was quite possible for a man to have an extensive knowledge of value theory and its copious refinements and to be able to prattle

away at great length about the rate of interest and its
possible "causes", without ever having realised the
fundamental part played by prices, costs, and interest
rates in the organisation of production.

In the modern treatment this is impossible. In the
modern treatment, discussion of "production" is an
integral part of the theory of equilibrium. It is shown
how factors of production are distributed between the
production of different goods by the mechanism of
prices and costs, how given certain fundamental data,
interest rates and price margins determine the distribution of factors between production for the present
and production for the future.[1] The doctrine of division
of labour, heretofore so disagreeably technological,
becomes an integral feature of a theory of moving
equilibrium through time. Even the question of "internal" organisation and administration now becomes
related to an outside network of relative prices and
costs; and since this is how things work in practice,
what is at first sight the greater remoteness of pure
theory in fact brings us much nearer to reality.

[1] The best discussions are to be found in Wicksell, *Lectures on Political
Economy*, vol.i., pp. 100-206 ; Hans Mayer, *Produktion* in the *Handwörterbuch
der Staatswissenschaften*.

CHAPTER IV

THE NATURE OF ECONOMIC GENERALISATIONS

1. WE have now sufficiently discussed the subject-matter of Economics and the fundamental conceptions associated therewith. But we have not yet discussed the nature of the generalisations whereby these conceptions are related. We have not yet discussed the nature and derivation of economic laws. This, therefore, is the purpose of the present chapter. When it is completed we shall be in a position to proceed to our second main task—investigation of the limitations and significance of this system of generalisations.

2. It is the object of this essay to arrive at conclusions which are based on the inspection of Economic Science as it actually exists. Its aim is not to discover how Economics should be pursued—that controversy, although we shall have occasion to refer to it *en passant*,[1] may be regarded as settled as between reasonable people—but rather what significance is to be attached to the results which it has already achieved. It will be convenient, therefore, at the outset of our investigations, if, instead of attempting to derive the nature of economic generalisations from the pure categories of our subject-

---

[1] See below, Section 4, and Chapter V., Section 3.

matter,[1] we proceed rather by examining specimens drawn from the existing body of analysis.

The most fundamental propositions of economic analysis are the propositions of the general theory of value. No matter what particular "school" is in question, no matter what arrangement of subject-matter is adopted, the body of propositions explaining the nature and the determination of the relation between given goods of the first order will be found to have a pivotal position in the whole system. It would be premature to say that the theory of this part of the subject is complete. But it is clear that enough has been done to warrant our taking the central propositions as established. We may proceed, therefore, to inquire on what their validity depends.

It should not be necessary to spend much time showing that it cannot rest upon a mere appeal to "History". The frequent concomitance of certain phenomena in time may suggest a problem to be solved. It cannot by itself be taken to imply a definite causal relationship. It might be shown that, whenever the conditions postulated in any of the simple corollaries of the theory of value have actually existed, the consequences deduced have actually been observed to follow. Thus, whenever the fixing of prices in relatively free markets has taken place it has been followed either by evasion or by the kind of distributive chaos which we associate with the food queues of the late war or the French or Russian Revolutions.[2] But this would not prove that the phenomena in question

[1] For an example of such a derivation reaching substantially similar results, see Strigl, *op. cit.*, p. 121 *seq.*

[2] If any reader of this book has any doubt of the evidence of the facts, he should consult the standard work on recent British experiments in such measures, *British Food Control*, by Sir William Beveridge.

were causally connected in any intimate sense. Nor would it afford any safe ground for predictions with regard to their future relationship. In the absence of rational grounds for supposing intimate connection, there would be no sufficient reason for supposing that history "would repeat itself". For if there is one thing which *is* shown by history, not less than by elementary logic, it is that historical induction, unaided by the analytical judgment, is the worst possible basis of prophecy.[1] "History shows", commences the bore at the club, and we resign ourselves to the prediction of the improbable. It is one of the great merits of the modern philosophy of history that it has repudiated all claims of this sort, and indeed makes it the *fundamentum divisionis* between history and natural science that history does not proceed by way of generalising abstraction.[2]

It is equally clear that our belief does not rest upon the results of controlled experiment. It is perfectly true that the particular case just mentioned has on more than one occasion been exemplified by the results of government intervention carried out under conditions which might be held to bear some resemblance to the conditions of controlled experiment. But it would be very superficial to suppose that the results of these "experiments" can be held to justify a proposition of such wide applicability, let alone the central

[1] "The vulgar notion that the safe methods on political subjects are those of Baconian induction—that the true guide is not general reasoning but specific experience—will one day be quoted as among the most unequivocal marks of a low state of the speculative faculties of any age in which it is accredited. . . . Whoever makes use of an argument of this kind . . . should be sent back to learn the elements of some one of the more easy physical sciences. Such reasoners ignore the fact of Plurality of Causes in the very case which affords the most signal example of it" (John Stuart Mill, *Logic*, chapter x., paragraph 8).

[2] See Rickert, *op. cit.*, pp. 78-101, *Die Grenzen der naturwissenschaftlichen Begriffsbildung, passim.* See also Max Weber, *op. cit., passim.*

propositions of the general theory of value. Certainly it would be a very fragile body of economic generalisations which could be erected on a basis of this sort. Yet, in fact, our belief in these propositions is as complete as belief based upon any number of controlled experiments.

But on what, then, does it depend?

It does not require much knowledge of modern economic analysis to realise that the foundation of the theory of value is the assumption that the different things that the individual wants to do have a different importance to him, and can be arranged therefore in a certain order. This notion can be expressed in various ways and with varying degrees of precision, from the simple want systems of Menger and the early Austrians to the more refined scales of relative valuations of Wicksteed and Schönfeld and the indifference systems of Pareto and Messrs. Hicks and Allen. But in the last analysis it reduces to this, that we can judge whether different possible experiences are of equivalent or greater or less importance to us. From this elementary fact of experience we can derive the idea of the substitutability of different goods, of the demand for one good in terms of another, of an equilibrium distribution of goods between different uses, of equilibrium of exchange and of the formation of prices. As we pass from the description of the behaviour of the single individual to the discussion of markets we naturally make other subsidiary assumptions—there are two individuals or many, the supply is in the hands of a monopoly or of a multiplicity of sellers, the individuals in one part of the market know or do not know what is going on in other parts of the market, the legal framework of the market prohibits this or that mode of acquisition or exchange, and so on. We assume, too, a given initial distribution of property.[1] But always the main underlying assumption is the assumption of the schemes of valuation of the different economic subjects. But this, we have seen already,[2] is really an assumption of one of the conditions which must be present if there is to be economic activity at all. It is an essential constituent of our conception of conduct with an economic aspect.

The propositions so far mentioned all relate to the theory of the valuation of given goods. In the elementary theory of value and exchange no inquiry is made into the conditions of continuous production. If we assume that production takes place, a new set of problems arises, necessitating new principles of explanation. We are confronted, *e.g.*, with the problem of explaining the relation between the value of the products and the value of the factors which produced them—the so-called problem of imputation. What is the sanction here for the solutions which have been put forward?

As is well known, the main principle of explanation, supplementary to the principles of subjective valuation assumed in the narrower theory of value and exchange, is the principle sometimes described as the Law of Diminishing Returns. Now the Law of Diminishing Returns is simply one way of putting the obvious fact that different factors of production are imperfect substitutes for one another. If you increase the amount of labour without increasing the amount of land the product will increase, but it will not in-

---

[1] On all this see the illuminating observations of Dr. Strigl, *Die ökonomischen Kategorien und die Organisation der Wirtschaft,* pp. 85-121.

[2] See above, Chapter I., Section 3.

crease proportionately. To secure a doubling of the product, if you do not double both land and labour, you have to more than double either one of the factors. This is obvious. If it were not so, then all the corn in the world could be produced from one acre of land. It follows, too, from considerations more intimately connected with our fundamental conceptions. A class of scarce factors is to be defined as consisting of those factors which are perfect substitutes. That is to say, difference in factors is to be defined essentially as imperfect substitutability. The Law of Diminishing Returns, therefore, follows from the assumption that there is more than one class of scarce factors of production.[1] The supplementary principle that, within limits, returns may increase, follows equally directly from the assumption that factors are relatively indivisible. On the basis of these principles and with the aid of subsidiary assumptions of the kind already mentioned (the nature of markets and the legal framework of production, etc.), it is possible to build up a theory of equilibrium of production.[2]

Let us turn to more dynamic considerations. The theory of profits, to use the word in the rather restricted sense in which it has come to be used in recent theory, is essentially an analysis of the effects of uncertainty with regard to the future availability of scarce goods and scarce factors. We live in a world in which, not only are the things that we want scarce,

[1] See Robinson, *Economics of Imperfect Competition*, pp. 330-31. I myself first learnt this way of putting things from a conversation with Professor Mises many years ago. But so far as I know Mrs. Robinson is the first to put matters so succinctly and clearly in print: I think that Mrs. Robinson's book will have done much to convince many hitherto sceptics of the utility and significance of the kind of abstract reasoning from very simple postulates which is the subject of the present discussion.

[2] See, *e.g.*, Schneider, *Theorie des Produktion, passim.*

but their exact occurrence is a matter of doubt and conjecture. In planning for the future we have to choose, not between certainties, but rather between a range of estimated probabilities. It is clear that the nature of this range itself may vary, and accordingly there must arise not only relative valuation of the different kinds of uncertainties between themselves, but also of different ranges of uncertainty similarly compared. From such concepts may be deduced many of the most complicated propositions of the theory of economic dynamics.[1]

And so we could go on. We could show how the use of money can be deduced from the existence of indirect exchange and how the demand for money can be deduced from the existence of the same uncertainties that we have just examined.[2] We could examine the propositions of the theory of capital and interest, and reduce them to elementary concepts of the type we have been here discussing. But it is unnecessary to prolong the discussion further. The examples we have already examined should be sufficient to establish the solution for which we are seeking. The propositions of economic theory, like all scientific theory, are obviously deductions from a series of postulates. And the chief of these postulates are all assumptions involving in some way simple and indisputable facts of experience relating to the way in which the scarcity of goods which is the subject-matter of our science actually shows itself in the world of reality. The main postulate of the theory of value is the fact that individuals can

[1] See Knight, *Risk, Uncertainty, and Profit*; Hicks, *The Theory of Profit* (*Economica*, No. 31, pp. 170-190).

[2] See Mises, *The Theory of Money*, pp. 147 and 200; Lavington, *The English Capital Market*, pp. 29-35; Hicks, *A Suggestion for Simplifying the Theory of Money* (*Economica*, 1934, pp. 1-20).

arrange their preferences in an order, and in fact do so. The main postulate of the theory of production is the fact that there are more than one factor of production. The main postulate of the theory of dynamics is the fact that we are not certain regarding future scarcities. These are not postulates the existence of whose counterpart in reality admits of extensive dispute once their nature is fully realised. We do not need controlled experiments to establish their validity: they are so much the stuff of our everyday experience that they have only to be stated to be recognised as obvious. Indeed, the danger is that they may be thought to be so obvious that nothing significant can be derived from their further examination. Yet in fact it is on postulates of this sort that the complicated theorems of advanced analysis ultimately depend. And it is from the existence of the conditions they assume that the general applicability of the broader propositions of economic science is derived.

3. Now of course it is true, as we have already seen, that the development of the more complicated applications of these propositions involves the use of a great multitude of subsidiary postulates regarding the condition of markets, the number of parties to the exchange, the state of the law, the *minimum sensible*[1] of buyers and sellers, and so on and so forth. The truth of the deductions from this structure depends, as always, on their logical consistency. Their applicability to the interpretation of any particular situation depends upon the existence in that situation of the elements postulated. Whether the theory of competition or of monopoly is applicable to a given situation is a matter for inquiry. As in the applica-

[1] See below, p. 99.

tions of the broad principles of the natural sciences, so
in the application of economic principles we must be
careful to enquire concerning the nature of our
material. It is not assumed that any of the many possible forms of competitive or monopolistic conditions
must necessarily always exist. But while it is important
to realise how many are the subsidiary assumptions
which necessarily arise as our theory becomes more
and more complicated, it is equally important to realise
how widely applicable are the main assumptions on
which it rests. As we have seen, the chief of them are
applicable whenever and wherever the conditions
which give rise to economic phenomena are present.

Considerations of this sort, it may be urged. should
enable us easily to detect the fallacy implicit in a
view which has played a great rôle in continental discussions. It has sometimes been asserted that the
generalisations of Economics are essentially "historico-
relative" in character, that their validity is limited
to certain historical conditions, and that outside these
they have no relevance to the analysis of social
phenomena. This view is a dangerous misapprehension.
It can be given plausibility only by a distortion of the
use of words so complete as to be utterly misleading.
It is quite true that in order fruitfully to apply the more
general propositions of Economics, it is important to
supplement them with a series of subsidiary postulates
drawn from the examination of what may often be
legitimately designated historico-relative material. It
is certain that unless this is done bad mistakes are
likely to be made. But it is not true that the main
assumptions are historico-relative *in the same sense*.
It is true that they are based upon experience, that
they refer to reality. But it is experience of so wide a

degree of generality as to place them in quite a different
class from the more properly designated historico-
relative assumptions. No one will really question the
universal applicability of such assumption as the
existence of scales of relative valuation, or of different
factors of production, or of different degrees of uncertainty regarding the future, even though there may
be room for dispute as to the best mode of describing
their exact logical status. And no one who has
really examined the kind of deductions which can
be drawn from such assumptions can doubt the
utility of starting from this plane. It is only failure
to realise this, and a too exclusive preoccupation with
the subsidiary assumptions, which can lend any
countenance to the view that the laws of Economics
are limited to certain conditions of time and space,
that they are purely historical in character, and so on.
If such views are interpreted to mean merely that we
must realise that the applications of general analysis
involve a host of subsidiary assumptions of a less
general nature, that before we apply our general
theory to the interpretation of a particular situation
we must be sure of the facts—well and good. Any
teacher who has watched good students over-in-
toxicated with the excitement of pure theory will
agree. It may even be conceded that at times there
may have been this degree of justification in the criticisms of the classical economists by the better sort of
historian. But if, as in the history of the great methodological controversies has notoriously been the case,
they are interpreted to mean that the broad conclusions springing from general analysis are as limited as
their particular applications—that the generalisations
of Political Economy were applicable only to the state

6

of England in the early part of the reign of Queen
Victoria, and such-like contentions—then it is clearly
utterly misleading. There is perhaps a sense in which
it is true to say that *all* scientific knowledge is
historico-relative. Perhaps in some other existence
it would all be irrelevant. But if this is so, then we
need a new term to designate what is usually called
historico-relative. So with that body of knowledge
which is general economics. If it is historico-relative, then a new term is needed to describe what we
know as historico-relative studies.

Stated this way, surely the case for the point of
view underlying the so-called "orthodox" conception
of the science since the time of Senior and Cairnes is
overwhelmingly convincing. It is difficult to see why
there should have been such fuss, why anybody should
have thought it worth while calling the whole position
in question. And, of course, if we examine the actual
history of the controversy it becomes abundantly
clear that the case for the attack was not primarily
scientific and philosophical at all. It may have been
the case that from time to time a sensitive historian
was outraged by the crudities of some very second-
rate economist—more probably by some business
man or politician repeating at second-hand what he
thought the economists had said. It may have been
the case sometimes that a pure logician has been
offended by an incautious use of philosophical terms on
the part of an economist, anxious to vindicate a body
of knowledge which he knows to be true and important. But in the main the attacks have not come
from these quarters. Rather they have been *political*
in nature. They have come from men with an axe to
grind—from men who wished to pursue courses which

the acknowledgment of law in the economic sphere would have suggested to be unwise. This was certainly the case with the majority of the leaders of the younger Historical School,[1] who were the spearhead of the attack on international liberalism in the Bismarckian era. It is equally the case to-day with the lesser schools which adopt a similar attitude. The only difference between Institutionalism and *Historismus* is that *Historismus* is much more interesting.

4. If the argument which has been developed above is correct, economic analysis turns out to be as Fetter has emphasised,[2] the elucidation of the implications of the necessity of choice in various assumed circumstances. In pure Mechanics we explore the implication of the existence of certain given properties of bodies. In pure Economics we examine the implication of the existence of scarce means with alternative uses. As we have seen, the assumption of relative valuations is the foundation of all subsequent complications.

It is sometimes thought, even at the present day, that this notion of relative valuation depends upon the validity of particular psychological doctrines. The borderlands of Economics are the happy hunting-ground of minds averse to the effort of exact thought, and, in these ambiguous regions, in recent years, endless time has been devoted to attacks on the alleged psychological assumptions of Economic Science. Psychology, it is said, advances very rapidly. If, therefore, Economics rests upon particular psychological doctrines, there is no task more ready to hand than every five years or so to write sharp polemics showing that, since psychology has changed its fashion,

[1] *Cp.* Mises, *Kritik des Interventionismus*, pp. 55-90.
[2] *Economic Principles*, pp. ix and 12-21.

Economics needs "rewriting from the foundations upwards". As might be expected, the opportunity has not been neglected. Professional economists, absorbed in the exciting task of discovering new truth, have usually disdained to reply: and the lay public, ever anxious to escape the necessity of recognising the implications of choice in a world of scarcity, has allowed itself to be bamboozled into believing that matters, which are in fact as little dependent on the truth of fashionable psychology as the multiplication table, are still open questions on which the enlightened man, who, of course, is nothing if not a psychologist, must be willing to suspend judgment.

Unfortunately, in the past, incautious utterances on the part of economists themselves have sometimes afforded a pretext for these strictures. It is well known that certain of the founders of the modern subjective theory of value did in fact claim the authority of the doctrines of psychological hedonism as sanctions for their propositions. This was not true of the Austrians. From the beginning the Mengerian tables were constructed in terms which begged no psychological questions.[1] Böhm-Bawerk explicitly repudiated any affiliation with psychological hedonism; indeed, he went to infinite pains to avoid this kind of misconception.[2] But the names of Gossen and Jevons and Edgeworth, to say nothing of their English followers, are a sufficient reminder of a line of really competent economists who did make pretensions of this sort. Gossen's *Entwicklung der Gesetze des menschlichen Verkehrs* certainly invokes hedonistic postulates. Jevons in his *Theory of Political Economy* prefaces

---

[1] See Menger, *Grundsätze*, 1 Aufl., pp. 77-152.
[2] See *Positive Theorie des Kapitals*, 4ᵉ Auflage, pp. 232-246.

his theory of utility and exchange with a theory of pleasure and pain. Edgeworth commences his *Mathematical Psychics* with a section which urges the conception of "man as a pleasure machine".[1] Attempts have even been made to exhibit the law of diminishing marginal utility as a special case of the Weber-Fechner Law.[2]

But it is fundamentally important to distinguish between the actual practice of economists, and the logic which it implies, and their occasional *ex post facto* apologia. It is just this distinction which the critics of Economic Science fail to make. They inspect with supererogatory zeal the external façade, but they shrink from the intellectual labour of examining the inner structure. Nor do they trouble to acquaint themselves with the more recent formulations of the theory they are attacking. No doubt this has strategic advantages, for, in polemics of this kind, honest misconception is an excellent spur to effective rhetoric; and no one who was acquainted with recent value theory could honestly continue to argue that it has any essential connection with psychological hedonism, or for that matter with any other brand of *Fach-Psychologie*. If the psychological critics of Economics had troubled to do these things they would speedily have perceived that the hedonistic trimmings of the works of Jevons and his followers were incidental to the main structure of a theory which—as the parallel development in Vienna showed—is capable of being set out and defended in absolutely non-hedonistic terms. As we have seen already, all that is assumed

[1] *Mathematical Psychics*, p. 15.
[2] For a refutation of this view, see Max Weber, *Die Grenznutzenlehr und das psychophysische Grundgesetz* (*Archiv für Sozialwissenschaft und Sozialpolitik*, vol. xxix., 1909).

in the idea of the scales of valuation is that different
goods have different uses and that these different uses
have different significances for action, such that in a
given situation one use will be preferred before another
and one good before another. Why the human animal
attaches particular values in this sense to particular
things, is a question which we do not discuss. That
is quite properly a question for psychologists or perhaps even physiologists. All that we need to assume
as economists is the obvious fact that different possibilities offer different incentives, and that these incentives can be arranged in order of their intensity.[1] The
various theorems which may be derived from this
fundamental conception are unquestionably capable of
explaining a manifold of social activity incapable of
explanation by any other technique. But they do this,
not by assuming some particular psychology, but by
regarding the things which psychology studies as the
data of their own deductions. Here, as so often, the
founders of Economic Science constructed something
more universal in its application than anything that
they themselves claimed.

But now the question arises how far even this procedure is legitimate. It should be clear from all that
has been said already that although it is not true that
the propositions of analytical economics rest upon
any particular psychology, yet they do most unquestionably involve elements which are of a psychological
—or perhaps better said a psychical—nature. This,
indeed, is explicitly recognised in the name by which
they are sometimes known—the subjective or psychological theory of value; and, as we have seen, it is

---

[1] That this does not assume the possibility of measuring valuations has
been already sufficiently emphasised in Chapter III., Section 4. above.

clear that the foundation of this theory is a psychical fact, the valuations of the individual. In recent years, however, partly as a result of the influence of Behaviourism, partly as a result of a desire to secure the maximum possible austerity in analytical exposition, there have arisen voices urging that this framework of subjectivity should be discarded. Scientific method, it is urged, demands that we should leave out of account anything which is incapable of direct observation. We may take account of demand as it shows itself in observable behaviour in the market. But beyond this we may not go. Valuation is a subjective process. We cannot *observe* valuation. It is therefore out of place in a scientific explanation. Our theoretical constructions must assume observable data. Such, for instance, is the attitude of Professor Cassel,[1] and there are passages in the later work of Pareto[2] which permit of a similar interpretation. It is an attitude which is very frequent among those economists who have come under the influence of Behaviourist psychology or who are terrified of attack from exponents of this queer cult.

At first sight this seems very plausible. The argument that we should do nothing that is not done in the physical sciences is very seductive. But it is doubtful whether it is really justified. After all, our business is to explain certain aspects of conduct. And it is very questionable whether this can be done in terms which involve no psychical element. It is quite certain that whether it be pleasing or no to the desire for the maximum austerity, we do in fact *understand* terms such as choice, indifference, preference, and the

[1] *The Theory of Social Economy*, First English Edition, vol. i., pp. 50-51.

[2] Notably in the article on *Economie mathématique* in the *Encyclopédie des Sciences mathématiques*, Paris, 1911.

like in terms of inner experience. The idea of an end, which is fundamental to our conception of the economic, is not possible to define in terms of external behaviour only. If we are to explain the relationships which arise from the existence of a scarcity of means in relation to a multiplicity of ends, surely at least one-half of the equation, as it were, must be psychical in character.

Such considerations would be decisive so long as it were taken for granted that the definition of the subject-matter of Economics suggested in this essay was correct. But it might be urged that they were simply an argument for rejecting that definition and substituting one relating only to "objective", observable matters, market prices, ratios of exchange, and so on. This is clearly what is implied by Professor Cassel's procedure—the celebrated *Ausschaltung der Wertlehre*.

But even if we restrict the object of Economics to the explanation of such observable things as prices, we shall find that in fact it is impossible to explain them unless we invoke elements of a subjective or psychological nature. It is surely clear, as soon as it is stated specifically, that the most elementary process of price determination must depend *inter alia* upon what people think is going to happen to prices in the future. The demand functions which Professor Cassel thinks enable us to dispense with any subjective elements, must be conceived not merely as relating to prices which prevail now, or which might prevail, on present markets, but also as relating to a whole series of prices which people expect to prevail in the future. It is obvious that what people expect to happen in the future is not susceptible of observation by purely behaviourist methods. Yet, as Professor Knight and others have shown, it is absolutely essential to take such anticipations into account if we are to understand at all the mechanics of economic change. It is essential for a thorough explanation of competitive prices. It is indispensable for the most superficial explanation of monopolistic prices. It is quite easy to exhibit such anticipations as part of a general system of scales of preference.[1] But if we suppose that such a system takes account of observable data only we deceive ourselves. How can we observe what a man thinks is going to happen?

It follows, then, that if we are to do our job as economists, if we are to provide a sufficient explanation of matters which every definition of our subject-matter necessarily covers, we must include psychological elements. They cannot be left out if our explanation is to be adequate. It seems, indeed, as if investigating this central problem of one of the most fully developed parts of any of the social sciences we have hit upon one of the essential differences between the social and the physical sciences. It is not the business of this essay to explore these more profound problems of methodology. But it may be suggested that if this case is at all typical—and some would regard the procedure of theory of prices as standing near the limit of proximity to the physical sciences— then the procedure of the social sciences which deal with conduct, which is in some sense purposive, can never be completely assimilated to the procedure of the physical sciences. It is really not possible to understand the concepts of choice, of the relationship of means and ends, the central concepts of our science, in

---

[1] See, e.g., Hicks, *Gleichgewicht und Konjunktur* (*Zeitschrift für National-ökonomie*, vol. iv., pp. 441-455).

terms of observation of external data. The conception of purposive conduct in this sense does not necessarily involve any ultimate indeterminism. But it does involve links in the chain of causal explanation which are psychical, not physical, and which are, for that reason, not necessarily susceptible of observation by behaviourist methods. Recognition of this does not in the least imply renunciation of "objectivity" in Max Weber's sense. It was exactly this that Max Weber had in mind when he wrote his celebrated essays.[1] All that the "objective" (that is to say, the *wertfrei*, to use Max Weber's phrase) explanation of conduct involves is the consideration of certain data, individual valuations, etc., which are not merely physical in character. The fact that such data are themselves of the nature of judgments of value does not necessitate that they should be valued as such. They are not judgments of value by the observer. What is of relevance to the social sciences is, not whether individual judgments of value are *correct* in the ultimate sense of the philosophy of value, but whether they are *made* and whether they are essential links in the chain of causal explanation. If the argument of this section is correct, this question must be answered in the affirmative.

5. But now the question arises whether the generalisations of economics, in addition to being based on this fundamental assumption of relative valuations, do not also depend upon a more general psychological assumption—upon the assumption of completely rational conduct. Is it not correct to de-

---

[1] Max Weber, *Die Objectivität socialwissenschaftlichen und socialpolitischen Erkenntnis : Der Sinn der Wertfreiheit der soziologischen und ökonomischen Wissenschaft* in *Gesammelte Aufsatze zur Wissenschaftlehre.*

scribe the subject-matter of Economics as the *rational disposal of goods*?[1] And in this sense cannot Economics be said to depend upon another, and more contentious, kind of psychological assumption than any we have yet examined? This is a matter of some intricacy which deserves attention, not only for its own sake, but for the light it casts upon the methods of Economics in general.

Now in so far as the idea of rational action involves the idea of *ethically appropriate* action, and it certainly is sometimes used in this sense in everyday discussion, it may be said at once—there will be more to be said about it later—that no such assumption enters into economic analysis. As we have just seen, economic analysis is *wertfrei* in the Weber sense. The values of which it takes account are valuations of individuals. The question whether in any further sense they are *valuable* valuations is not one which enters into its scope. If the word rationality is to be construed as in any way implying this meaning, then it may be said that the concept for which it stands does not enter into economic analysis.

But in so far as the term rational is taken to mean merely "consistent", then it is true that an assumption of this sort does enter into certain analytical constructions. The celebrated generalisation that in a state of equilibrium the relative significance of divisible

---

[1] In her interesting pamphlet entitled *Economics is a Serious Subject* Mrs. Joan Robinson reproaches me for not having made this limitation. (The word she uses is "sensible", but I do not think she would dispute my interpretation of her meaning.) I had, indeed, in various phrases tucked away a negative attitude to such a proposal. But I did not deal with it explicitly for fear of being charged with the introduction of overmuch discussion of side issues. I now see that this was wrong. The following section is an attempt to deal more positively with this question. But it is a matter of very great difficulty to put things correctly, and I am far from claiming to have provided a definitive analysis.

commodities is equal to their price. does involve the
assumption that each final choice is consistent with
every other, in the sense that if I prefer A to B and
B to C, I also prefer A to C: in short, that in a state
of perfect equilibrium the possibility of advantage from
further "internal arbitrage operations" is excluded.

There is a wider sense, too, in which the conception
of rationality as equivalent to consistency can be understood as figuring in discussions of the conditions of
equilibrium. It may be irrational to be completely
consistent as between commodities, in the sense just
described, just because the time and attention which
such exact comparisons require are (in the opinion of
the economic subject concerned) better spent in other
ways. In other words, there may be an opportunity
cost of "internal arbitrage" which, beyond a certain
point, outweighs the gain. The marginal utility of
not bothering about marginal utility is a factor of
which account has been taken by the chief writers
on the subjective theory of value from Böhm-Bawerk
onwards. It is not a recent discovery. It can be taken
into account in a formal sense by permitting a certain
margin (or structure of margins) of inconsistency between particular valuations.

It is perfectly true that the assumption of perfect
rationality figures in constructions of this sort. But it
is not true that the generalisations of economics are
limited to the explanation of situations in which action
is perfectly consistent. Means may be scarce in relation to ends, even though the ends be inconsistent.
Exchange, production, fluctuation—all take place in
a world in which people do not know the full implications of what they are doing. It is often inconsistent
(*i.e.*, irrational in this sense) to wish at once for the

fullest satisfaction of consumers' demands, and at the same time to impede the import of foreign goods by tariffs or such-like obstacles. Yet it is frequently done: and who shall say that economic science is not competent to explain the situation resulting?

Of course there is a sense in which the word rationality can be used which renders it legitimate to argue that at least some rationality is assumed before human behaviour has an economic aspect—the sense, namely, in which it is equivalent to "purposive". As we have seen already, it is arguable that if behaviour is not conceived of as purposive, then the conception of the means-end relationships which economics studies has no meaning. So if there were no purposive action, it could be argued that there were no economic phenomena.[1] But to say this is not to say in the least that all purposive action is completely consistent. It may indeed be urged that the more that purposive action becomes conscious of itself, the more it necessarily becomes consistent. But this is not to say that it is necessary to assume *ab initio* that it always is consistent or that the economic generalisations are limited to that, perhaps, tiny section of conduct where all inconsistencies have been resolved.

The fact is, of course, that the assumption of perfect

---

[1] It is in this sense, I think, that Professor Mises uses the term when he argues that all *conduct* (Handeln) must be conceived of as rational as opposed to merely vegetative reactions (*Grundprobleme der Nationalökonomie*, pp. 22 and 34). The great emphasis which Professor Mises has laid upon this use of the term follows necessarily from his insistence that for the purposes of the social sciences conduct is not to be divided according to ethical standards. That is, that it is not to be divided into *rational* and *irrational* using these terms with a normative significance. Those who have criticised Professor Mises, on the assumption that he uses the word in other senses, have really not paid sufficient attention to the context of his emphasis. It is surely gratuitous to assume that the author of the *Kritik des Interventionismus* has omitted to notice that conduct may be irrational in the sense of *inconsistent*.

rationality in the sense of complete consistency is simply one of a number of assumptions of a psychological nature which are introduced into economic analysis at various stages of approximation to reality. The perfect foresight, which it is sometimes convenient to postulate, is an assumption of a similar nature. The purpose of these assumptions is not to foster the belief that the world of reality corresponds to the constructions in which they figure, but rather to enable us to study, in isolation, tendencies which, in the world of reality, operate only in conjunction with many others, and then, by contrast as much as by comparison, to turn back to apply the knowledge thus gained to the explanations of more complicated situations. In this respect, at least, the procedure of pure economics has its counterpart in the procedure of all physical sciences which have gone beyond the stage of collection and classification.

6. Considerations of this sort enable us to deal also with the oft-reiterated accusation that Economics assumes a world of economic men concerned only with money-making and self-interest. Foolish and exasperating as this may appear to any competent economist, it is worth some further examination. Although it is false, yet there is a certain expository device of pure analysis which, if not explained in detail, might give rise to strictures of this nature.

The general absurdity of the belief that the world contemplated by the economist is peopled only by egotists or "pleasure machines" should be sufficiently clear from what has been said already. The fundamental concept of economic analysis is the idea of relative valuations; and, as we have seen, while we assume that different goods have different values at different margins, we do not regard it as part of our problem to explain why these particular valuations exist. We take them as data. So far as we are concerned, our economic subjects can be pure egoists, pure altruists, pure ascetics, pure sensualists or—what is much more likely—mixed bundles of all these impulses. The scales of relative valuation are merely a convenient formal way of exhibiting certain permanent characteristics of man as he actually is. Failure to recognise the primacy of these valuations is simply a failure to understand the significance of the last sixty years of Economic Science.

Now the valuations which determine particular transactions may be of various degrees of complexity. In my purchase of bread I may be interested solely in the comparison between the bread and the other things in the circle of exchange on which I might have spent the money. But I may be interested too in the happiness of my baker. There may exist between us certain liens which make it preferable for me to buy bread from him, rather than procure it from his competitor who is willing to sell it a little cheaper. In exactly the same way, in my sale of my own labour or the hire of my property, I may be interested only in the things which I receive as a result of the transaction; or I may be interested also in the experience of labouring in one way rather than another, or in the prestige or discredit, the feeling of virtue or shame in hiring out my property in this line rather than in that.

All these things are taken into account in our conception of scales of relative valuation. And the generalisations descriptive of economic equilibrium are couched in a form which explicitly brings this to the fore. Every first-year student since the days of Adam Smith has learnt to describe equilibrium in the distribution of particular grades of labour in terms of a tendency, *not* to the maximisation of *money gains*, but to the maximisation of *net advantages* in the various alternatives open.[1] As we have seen already, the theory of risk, too, and its influence on the capital market depends essentially on assumptions of this kind. But sometimes for purposes of exposition it is convenient to start from the first approximation that the valuation is of a very simple order, and that, on the one side is a thing desired or offered, and on the other is the money to be got or given in exchange for it. For the elucidation of certain complicated propositions, such as the theory of costs or marginal productivity analysis, it permits an economy of terms. It is not in the least difficult, at the appropriate stage, to remove these assumptions and to pass to analysis couched in terms of complete generality.

This, then, is all that lies behind the *homo œconomicus*—the occasional assumption that in certain exchange relationships all the means, so to speak, are on one side and all the ends on the other. If, *e.g.*, for purposes of demonstrating the circumstances in which a single price will emerge in a limited market, it is assumed that in my dealings in that market I always buy from the cheapest seller, it is not assumed at all that I am necessarily actuated by egotistical motives. On the contrary, it is well known that the impersonal relationship postulated is to be seen in its purest form

---

[1] See Cantillon, *Essai sur la Nature du Commerce* (Higgs' edition), p. 21; Adam Smith, *Wealth of Nations*, Bk. I., ch. x; Senior, *Political Economy*, pp. 200-216; McCulloch, *Political Economy*, pp. 364-378; J. S. Mill, *Political Economy*, 5th edition, vol. i., pp. 460-483; Marshall, *Principles*, 8th edition, pp. 546-558—to take a representative sample of what would be regarded as the more hard-boiled English tradition. For an up-to-date version of these doctrines, see Wicksteed, *Commonsense of Political Economy*, Part I., *passim*.

when trustees, not being in a position to allow themselves the luxury of more complicated relationships, are trying to make the best terms for the estates they administer: your business man is a much more complicated fellow. All that it means is that my relation to the dealers does not enter into my hierarchy of ends. For me (who may be acting for myself or my friends or some civic or charitable authority) they are regarded merely as means. Or, again, if it is assumed—which in fact is usually done for purposes of showing *by contrast* what the total influences in equilibrium bring about—that I sell my labour always in the dearest market, it is not assumed that money and self-interest are my ultimate objects —I may be working entirely to support some philanthropic institution. It is assumed only that, so far as that transaction is concerned, my labour is only a means to an end; it is not to be regarded as an end in itself.

If this were commonly known, if it were generally realised that Economic Man is only an expository device—a first approximation used very cautiously at one stage in the development of arguments which, in their full development, neither employ any such assumption nor demand it in any way for a justification of their procedure—it is improbable that he would be such a universal bogey. But of course it is generally thought that he has a wider significance, that he lurks behind all those generalisations of the "Laws of Supply and Demand" better described as the theory of comparative statics, whose elucidation so often is inimical to the desire to be able to believe it to be possible both to have your cake and to eat it. And it is for this reason that he is so furiously attacked. If it were

7

Economic Man who barred the gates of Cloud-cuckoo-land, then it might well seem that a little psychology —it would not matter much of what brand—might be expected to burst them open. What prestige, what repute for really *deep* insight into human motivation might be expected to accrue from so spectacular an exposure!

Unfortunately this belief rests upon misapprehension. The propositions of the theory of variations do not involve the assumption that men are actuated *only* by considerations of money gains and losses. They involve only the assumption that money plays *some* part in the valuation of the given alternatives. And they suggest only that if from any position of equilibrium the money incentive is *varied* this must tend to alter the equilibrium valuations. Money may not be regarded as playing a predominant part in the situation contemplated. So long as it plays some part then the propositions are applicable.

A simple illustration should make this quite plain. Let us suppose that a small bounty is granted in respect of the production of an article produced under conditions of free competition. According to well-known theorems there will be a tendency for the production of that commodity to increase—the magnitude of the increase depending upon considerations of elasticity into which it is not necessary for us to enter. Now upon what does this generalisation depend? Upon the assumption that producers are actuated only by considerations of monetary gain? Not at all. We may assume that they take into account all the "other advantages and disadvantages" with which Cantillon and Adam Smith have made us familiar. But, if we assume that before the bounty was granted

there was equilibrium, we must assume that its institution must disturb the equilibrium. The granting of
the bounty implies a lowering of the terms on which
real income is obtainable in this particular line of
enterprise. It is a very elementary proposition that
if a price is lowered the demand tends to increase.

There is perhaps one refinement of this conclusion
which needs to be stated explicitly. It may quite well
be that, if the change contemplated is a very small
one, no primary movement will take place.[1] Is this in
contradiction with our theory? Not at all. The idea
of scales of valuation does not assume that every
physical unit of any of the things which enter into the
range of effective valuation must necessarily have a
separate significance for action. In the assumption of
the hierarchy of alternatives we do not ignore the fact
that, for change to be effective, it must attain the
minimum sensibile.[2] Changes in price of a penny or
twopence may not affect the habits of a given economic
subject. But this is not to say that changes of a
shilling will not be effective. Nor is it to say that,
given limited resources, the necessity of spending more
or less on one thing does not *inevitably* affect the
distribution of expenditure, even if in the line of
expenditure directly affected it leaves the quantity
demanded unchanged.

7. In the light of all that has been said the nature
of economic analysis should now be plain. It consists
of deductions from a series of postulates, the chief of
which are almost universal facts of experience present

---

[1] By primary movement, I mean movement in the line of production
affected; by secondary movement, expansions or contractions of expenditure
in other lines. As argued below, some secondary movement is almost
inevitable.

[2] *Cp.* Wicksteed, *op. cit.*, Part II., chs. i. and ii.

whenever human activity has an economic aspect, the rest being assumptions of a more limited nature based upon the general features of particular situations or types of situations which the theory is to be used to explain.

It is sometimes thought, however, that such a conception is essentially statical in nature, that it relates only to descriptions of final positions of equilibrium, variations being essentially outside its scope. Since the world of reality is not in a state of equilibrium, but rather exhibits the appearance of incessant change, it follows that knowledge of this sort has little explanatory value. This belief, which apparently is very widespread, needs further examination.

Now it is quite true that the elementary propositions of economic analysis are descriptions of stationary equilibrium. We start by examining, not conditions of complete rest, as in the Statics from which by analogy the name of this part of our subject is sometimes taken, but conditions in which the various "flows" of activity exhibit no tendency to change, or change only in a recurrent cycle.[1] Thus we may take the conditions of a simple market in which the fundamental conditions of supply and demand are unaltered from day to day and enquire under what conditions would the quantities exchanged day by day remain invariable, even though the parties to the exchange

[1] In his interesting remarks on the relation between statics and dynamics (*Prolegomena to Relativity Economics*, pp. 11-13) Professor Souter appears to assume that the possibility of recurrent change within a stationary equilibrium is overlooked by those who operate with this concept. I venture to suggest that this is a misapprehension. Change of this sort has certainly been taken account of. Professor Schumpeter's description of a stationary society in the first chapter of his *Theory of Economic Development* certainly does not assume that corn is reaped all the year round, and the particular complications of this concept of intertemporal equilibrium have been very thoroughly examined by Professor Hayek in his article on the *Intertemporale Gleichgewicht System, Weltwirtschaftliches Archiv*, Bd. 28, pp. 33-76.

were free to vary their bargains. Or we may consider the case in which the production takes place, but in which the fundamental data—that is, the valuations of the economic subjects, the technical possibilities of production and the ultimate supplies of the factors—are unchanged, and enquire under what condition there would be no tendency to change in the rate of flow of products. And so on. There is no need to rehearse the whole list of possibilities; any of the more rigorous text-books on the subject—for instance, Wicksell's *Lectures on Political Economy*, or Walras' *Elements*—provide examples of the sort of thing under discussion.

But it is quite wrong to suppose that our investigations are limited to these essential preliminaries. Once we have thoroughly investigated the conditions of constant flows, and hence learnt *by contrast* to understand the conditions in which the flows will be tending to alter, we may push our investigations further and consider variations.

We may do this in two ways. In the first place, we may compare the equilibrium positions, assuming small variations in the data. Thus we may assume the imposition of a tax, the discovery of a change in technical methods, a change in tastes, and so on. And we may endeavour to ascertain in what respects one equilibrium position differs from the other. The so-called classical analysis, imperfect as a full description of final states of equilibrium, provides a great variety of useful comparisons of differences of this sort. This part of our theory has sometimes been called the theory of comparative statics.[1]

But we may go beyond this. Not only may we com-

---

[1] The phrase, I believe, is due to Dr. Schams. See his *Komparative Statik (Zeitschrift für Nationalökonomie*, Bd. II, pp. 27-61). But, as indicated above, the procedure goes back to the time of the classical economists.

pare two final states of equilibrium assuming given variations, we may also endeavour to trace out the path actually followed by different parts of a system if a state of disequilibrium is given. This, of course, is the significance of Marshall's "period" analysis. Into this category falls also much of what is most significant in the theory of money and banking. And in doing all this we make no assumption that final equilibrium is necessary. We assume that there are operative in different parts of the system certain tendencies which make for the restoration of an equilibrium in respect to certain limited points of reference. But we do not assume that the composite effect of these tendencies will necessarily be equilibrating. It is easy to conceive of initial configurations of the data, which have no total tendency to equilibrium, but which rather tend to cumulative oscillation.[1]

In all this, as will be obvious to anyone acquainted with the procedure of economic analysis, our knowledge of the statical foundations is fundamental.[2] We

---

[1] See the illuminating article of Dr. Rosenstein-Rodan, *The Rôle of Time in Economic Theory* (*Economica*, new series, vol. i., p. 77).

[2] Professor Souter has misconceived entirely my attitude to Marshall in this connection, doubtless on account of crudities in my exposition. I was once bold enough to say that I regarded the stationary state as a theoretical instrument as superior to the statical method (*On a Certain Ambiguity in the Conception of Stationary Equilibrium*, *Economic Journal*, vol. xl., p. 194). By this, however, I did *not* mean that I regarded the analysis of stationary equilibrium as an end in itself, and the dynamic investigations in the sense here indicated, which of course were Marshall's chief preoccupation, superfluous. I do most cordially agree with Professor Souter's high claims for Marshall here. In many respects we are only painfully regaining ground which he conquered thirty years ago. And I completely agree, as I have emphasised above, that the *raison d'être* of statical investigations is the explanation of dynamic change. All that I meant, in the sentences to which Professor Souter takes such strong exception, was that if we are to proceed to these dynamic investigations, we shall do so the better equipped if we are fully aware of all the implications of full stationary equilibrium than if we go simply on a knowledge gained from the examination of partial equilibrium positions. I agree that it would be wrong to speak as if Marshall was not aware of the intricacies of full interdependence, though I think he sometimes overlooked things here which subsequent investigations have brought to

examine change by comparing small differences of
equilibrium or by comparing the effects of different
tendencies to equilibrium; it is difficult to see what
other procedure could be adopted. But it should
be equally obvious that we study these statical
problems not merely for their own sake, but in order
to apply them to the explanation of change. There
are certain propositions of economic statics which are
significant and important in themselves. But it is
hardly an exaggeration to say that their chief significance lies in their further application in economic
dynamics. We study the laws of "rest" in order to
understand the laws of change.

But now the question arises, Can we not even
transcend all this? Will the dynamic operations described so far relate to the study of the effects of given
variations in the data, or the consequences of given
disequilibria? Can we not go outside all this and explain
changes in the data themselves? This raises questions
which can be treated more conveniently in another
chapter.

---

light, and I am inclined to agree that in order to study many kinds of change
we have to abstract—as did Marshall—from all the remote possibilities of
interdependence. But I do think that it is legitimate to argue that it is better
to do this, having explicitly recognised and stated all the difficulties, than to
proceed straight away to the dynamic problems, leaving the full statical
foundations to be provided intuitively by the reader. It is surely not derogating from the high esteem in which Marshall must be held by all sensible
people, to urge that Economics would be further advanced to-day than it
actually is if, instead of regarding them as a burden which his readers were to
be spared, he had rigorously set out all the assumptions of his procedure; we
have had to relearn so much that he did not think it worth while to set forth
explicitly. No doubt even this is a matter of opinion. It is easy to sympathise
with the desire to be comprehensible to competent members of the world of
affairs who, in spite of their competence, would be impatient of the severities
of rigorous analysis; and teachers at least must be grateful to Marshall for
having provided a work which will prevent beginners from being carried away
by facile mathematics. But it is difficult not to agree with Mr. Keynes that
it is a pity Marshall did not publish more monographs like the *Papers on the
Pure Theory of International and Domestic Values.* Would Professor Souter
really disagree with this?

CHAPTER V

ECONOMIC GENERALISATIONS AND REALITY

1. IT is a characteristic of scientific generalisations that they refer to reality. Whether they are cast in hypothetical or categorical form, they are distinguished from the propositions of pure logic and mathematics by the fact that in some sense their reference is to that which exists, or that which may exist, rather than to purely formal relations.

In this respect, it is clear, the propositions of Economics are on all fours with the proposition of all other sciences. As we have seen, these propositions are deductions from simple assumptions reflecting very elementary facts of general experience. If the premises relate to reality the deductions from them must have a similar point of reference.

It follows, therefore, that the belief often expressed by the critics of Economics, that it is a mere system of formal inferences having no necessary relation to reality, is based upon misconception. It may be admitted that our knowledge of the facts which are the basis of economic deductions is different in important respects from our knowledge of the facts which are the basis of the deductions of the natural sciences. It may be admitted, too, that for this reason the methods of economic science—although not the tests of its logical consistency—are often different from the methods of the natural sciences. But it does not follow in the least that its generalisations have a "merely formal" status—that they are "scholastic" deductions from arbitrarily established definitions. Indeed, it may be urged that, on the contrary, there is less reason to doubt their real bearing than that of the generalisations of the natural sciences. In Economics, as we have seen, the ultimate constituents of our fundamental generalisations are known to us by immediate acquaintance. In the natural sciences they are known only inferentially. There is much less reason to doubt the counterpart in reality of the assumption of individual preferences than that of the assumption of the electron.[1] It is true that we deduce much from definitions. But it is not true that the definitions are arbitrary.

It follows, too, that it is a complete mistake to regard the economist, whatever his degree of "purity", as concerned merely with pure deduction. It is quite true that much of his work is in the nature of elaborate processes of inference. But it is quite untrue to suppose that it is only, or indeed mainly, thus. The concern of the economist is the interpretation of reality. The business of discovery consists not merely in the elucidation of given premises but in the perception of the facts which are the basis of the premises. The process of discovering those elements in common experience which afford the basis of our trains of deductive reasoning is economic discovery just as much as the shaking out of new inferences from old premises. The theory of value as we know it has developed in

---

[1] See the classical discussion of this matter in Cairnes' *Character and Logical Method of Political Economy*, 2nd edition, pp. 81-99. See also Hayek: *Collectivist Economic Planning*, pp. 8-12.

recent times by the progressive elaboration of deductions from very simple premises. But the great discovery, the Mengerian revolution, which initiated this period of progress, was the discovery of the premises themselves. Similarly with the other foundations we have discussed. The perception and selection of the basis of economic analysis is as much economics as the analysis itself. Indeed it is this which gives analysis significance.

2. At the same time it must be admitted that the propositions which have hitherto been established are very general in character. If a certain good is scarce, then we know that its disposal must conform to certain laws. If its demand schedule is of a certain order, then we know that with alterations of supply its price must move in a certain way. But, as we have discovered already,[1] there is nothing in this conception of scarcity which warrants us in attaching it to any particular commodity. Our deductions do not provide any justification for saying that caviare is an economic good and carrion a disutility. Still less do they inform us concerning the intensity of the demand for caviare or the demand to be rid of carrion. From the point of view of pure Economics these things are conditioned on the one side by individual valuations, and on the other by the technical facts of the given situation. And both individual valuations and technical facts are outside the sphere of economic uniformity. To use Strigl's expressive phrase, from the point of view of economic analysis, these things constitute the *irrational* element in our universe of discourse.[2]

But is it not desirable to transcend such limita-

---

[1] See above, Chapter II., Sections 1, 2, 3.
[2] Strigl, *op. cit.*, p. 18.

tions? Ought we not to wish to be in a position to give numerical values to the scales of valuation, to establish quantitative laws of demand and supply? This raises, in a slightly different form, some of the questions we left unanswered at the conclusion of the last chapter.

No doubt such knowledge would be useful. But a moment's reflection should make it plain that we are here entering upon a field of investigation *where there is no reason to suppose that uniformities are to be discovered*. The "causes" which bring it about that the ultimate valuations prevailing at any moment are what they are, are heterogeneous in nature: there is no ground for supposing that the resultant effects should exhibit significant uniformity over time and space. No doubt there is a sense in which it can be argued that every random sample of the universe is the result of determinate causes. But there is no reason to suppose that the study of a random sample of random samples is likely to yield generalisations of any significance. That is not the procedure of the sciences. Yet that, or something very much like it, is the assumption underlying the expectation that the formal categories of economic analysis can be given substantial content of permanent and constant value.[1]

A simple illustration should make this quite clear. Let us take the demand for herrings. Suppose we are confronted with an order fixing the price of herrings at a point below the price hitherto ruling in the market. Suppose we were in a position to say, "According to the researches of Blank (1907-1908) the elasticity of demand for the common herring (*Clupea harengus*) is 1·3; the present price-fixing order therefore may be

[1] Note the qualification "permanent and constant value". Before the above conclusion is dismissed as too drastic, the remarks below on the positive value of investigations of this sort should be examined.

expected to leave an excess of demand over supply of two million barrels". How pleasant it would be to be able to say things like this! How flattering to our usually somewhat damaged self-esteem *vis-a-vis* the natural scientists!   How impressive to big business! How persuasive to the general public!

But can we hope to attain such an enviable position? Let us assume that in 1907-1908 Blank had succeeded in ascertaining that, with a given price change in that year, the elasticity of demand was 1·3. Rough computations of this sort are not really very difficult and may have considerable utility for certain purposes. But what reason is there to suppose that he was unearthing a constant law? No doubt the herring meets certain physiological needs which are capable of fairly accurate description, although it is by no means the only food capable of meeting these needs. The demand for herrings, however, is not a simple derivative of needs. It is, as it were, a function of a great many apparently independent variables. It is a function of fashion; and by fashion is meant something more than the ephemeral results of an Eat British Herrings campaign; the demand for herrings might be substantially changed by a change in the theological views of the economic subjects entering the market. It is a function of the availability of other foods. It is a function of the quantity and quality of the population. It is a function of the distribution of income within the community and of changes in the volume of money. Transport changes will alter the area of demand for herrings. Discoveries in the art of cooking may change their relative desirability. Is it possible reasonably to suppose that coefficients derived from the observation of a particular herring market at a

particular time and place have any *permanent* significance—save as Economic History?

Now, of course, by the aid of various devices it is
possible to extend the area of observation over periods
of time. Instead of observing the market for herrings
for a few days, statistics of price changes and changes
in supply and demand may be collected over a period
of years and by judicious "doctoring" for seasonal
movements, population change, and so on, be used to
deduce a figure representing average elasticity over
the period. And within limits such computations
have their uses. They are a convenient way of describing certain forces operative during that period of
history. As we shall see later on, they may provide
some guidance concerning what may happen in the
immediate future. Rough ideas relating to the elasticity of demand in particular markets are indeed
essential if we are to make full use of the more refined
tools of economic analysis. But they have no claim
to be regarded as immutable laws. However ac-
curately they describe the past, there is no presumption that they must continue to describe the future.
Things have just happened to be so in the past. They
may continue to be so for a short time in the future.
But there is no reason to suppose that their having
been so in the past is the result of the operation of
homogeneous causes, nor that their changes in the
future will be due to the causes which have operated
in the past. If we wanted to be helpful about herrings
we should never dream of relying on the researches of
the wretched Blank who was working in 1907-8. We
should work the whole thing out afresh on the basis
of more recent data. Important as such investigations
may be—and nothing that is here said on their method-

ological status should be regarded as derogating from their very considerable practical value—there is no justification for claiming for their results the status of the so-called "statistical" laws of the natural sciences.[1]

But, it might be said, is not the difference between the results of such investigation and the postulates on which, as was shown in the last chapter, the main generalisation of Economics depends, a matter only of *degree* rather than kind? It has been shown that if there were not a hierarchy of ends, but if the different ends were all of equal importance, the results of conduct would be quite indeterminate, and even the most elementary generalisations of the theory of value would not be applicable. There is no guarantee that this will not happen. It is only a matter of probability that the conditions making such propositions applicable will persist. In exactly the same way it can be shown analytically that circumstances are conceivable in which the demand curve may have a positive inclination. Yet if this were frequent many of the best accepted generalisations of deductive theory would not be applicable. Again, it is only a matter of probability that this is not the case. Wherein is the difference of kind between this assumption and the assumption that the elasticity of demand for herrings is 1·3?

The argument is weighty. And it may be freely conceded that in this sense the difference is a difference of degree rather than a difference of kind. But it is surely open to the reply that the difference of degree is so great as to justify our acting as if it were a

[1] On the problems discussed above very interesting remarks are to be found in Halberstaédter, *Die Problematik des wirtschaftlichen Prinzips*.

difference of kind. It *might* be the case that valuations were of such a peculiar nature that conduct was in-determinate. But it is so overwhelmingly unlikely that we are warranted in neglecting the possibility. It is not so unlikely that the demand function may be positive, but there is still a very strong probability that this is not the rule, but the exception. On the other hand, when we are dealing with the valuation of particular products and the elasticity of demand derived therefrom, for the reasons already set forth, there is surely an overwhelming probability that constancy is not to be expected. Here, indeed, we have the historico-relative *in excelsis*. The fact that we can arrange our preferences in an order is a fact of so much greater a degree of generality than the actual momentary order of preference of any individual that we are surely justified in regarding them as possessing, in our universe of discourse at least, a difference of status. And while it is arguable that in the future much valuable work will be done in attempting to ascertain these momentary values, it seems more important, if a sense of proportion is to be maintained, that their limitations should be realised than that stress should be laid on the formal similarity with the broad qualita-tive foundations which constitute the basis of the science as we know it. Perhaps, indeed, this is another of the methodological differences between the natural and the social sciences. In the natural sciences the transition from the qualitative to the quantitative is easy and inevitable. In the social sciences, for reasons which have already been set forth, it is in some connection almost impossible, and it is always as-sociated with peril and difficulty. It seems clear, from what has happened already, that less harm is likely to be done by emphasising the differences between the social and the natural sciences than by emphasising their similarities.[1]

3. If this is true of attempts to provide definite quantitative values for such elementary concepts as demand and supply functions, how much more does it apply to attempts to provide "concrete" laws of the movement of more complex phenomena, price fluctuations, cost dispersions, business cycles, and the like. In the last ten years there has been a great multiplication of this sort of thing under the name of Institutionalism, "Quantitative Economics", "Dynamic Economics", and what not;[2] yet most of the investigations involved have been doomed to futility from the outset and might just as well never have been undertaken. The theory of probability on which modern mathematical statistics is based affords no justification for averaging where conditions are obviously not such as to warrant the belief that homogeneous causes of different kinds are operating. Yet this is the normal procedure of much of the work of this kind. The correlation of trends subject to influences of the most diverse character is scrutinised for "quantitative laws". Averages are taken of phenomena occurring under the most heterogeneous circumstances of time and space, and the result is expected to have significance. In Professor Wesley Mitchell's *Business Cycles*,[3]

[1] On the matters discussed in this section I am much indebted to conversations with Dr. Machlup.

[2] On the aspect of Institutionalism discussed below, Professor Wesley Mitchell's essay on *The Prospects of Economics* in the *Trend of Economics* (edited Tugwell) should be consulted. On the general position of the school, see Morgenstern, *Bemerkungen über die Problematik der Amerikanischen Institutionalisten* in the *Saggi di Storia e Teoria Economica in onore e recordo di Giuseppe Prato*, Turin, 1931; Fetter, art. America, *Wirtschaftstheorie der Gegenwart*, Bd. 1, pp. 31-60. See also the review of the *Trend of Economics* by the late Professor Allyn Young, reprinted in his *Economic Problems New and Old*, pp. 232-260.   [3] *Business Cycles*, 2nd edition, p. 419.

for instance, a work for whose magnificent collection of data economists are rightly grateful, after a prolonged and valuable account of the course of business fluctuations in different countries since the end of the eighteenth century, an average is struck of the duration of all cycles and a logarithmic normal curve is fitted by Davies' Method to the frequency distribution of the 166 observations involved. What possible meaning can inhere in such an operation? Here are observations of conditions widely differing in time, space, and the institutional framework of business activity. If there is any significance at all in bringing them together, it must be by way of *contrast*. Yet Professor Mitchell, who never tires of belittling the methods and results of orthodox analysis, apparently thinks that, by taking them all together and fitting a highly complicated curve to their frequency distribution, he is constructing something significant—something which is more than a series of straight lines and curves on half a page of his celebrated treatise.[1] Certainly he has provided the most mordant comment on the methodology of "Quantitative Economics" that any of its critics could possibly wish.

There is no need to linger on the futility of these grandiose projects. After all, in spite of their recent popularity, they are not new, and a movement which has continually invoked a pragmatic logic may well be judged by a pragmatic test. It is just about a

[1] On this see Morgenstern, *International vergleichende Konjunktur-forschung* (*Zeitschrift für die Gesammte Staatswissenschaft*, vol.lxxxiii.,p.261). In the second edition of his book, Professor Mitchell attempts to meet Dr. Morgenstern's strictures in an extensive footnote, but so far as I can see, beyond urging that his observations for China relate to coast towns (!), he does not go beyond a reiteration that "the distribution of the observations around their central tendency is a matter of much theoretical interest" (*Business Cycles*, 2nd edition, p. 420).

hundred years ago since Richard Jones, in his Inaugural Lecture at King's College, London,[1] sounded the note of revolt against the "formal abstraction" of Ricardian Economics, with arguments which, if more vividly expressed, are more or less exactly similar to those which have been expressed by the advocates of "inductive methods" ever since that day. And time has gone on, and the "rebels" have become a highly respectable band of expert authorities, the pontifical occupants of chairs, the honoured recipients of letters from the Kaiser, the directing functionaries of expensive research institutes. . . . We have had the Historical School. And now we have the Institutionalists. Save in one or two privileged places, it is safe to say that, until the close of the War, views of this sort were dominant in German University circles; and in recent years, if they have not secured the upper hand altogether, they have certainly had a wide area of power in America. Yet not one single "law" deserving of the name, not one quantitative generalisation of permanent validity has emerged from their efforts. A certain amount of interesting statistical material. Many useful monographs on particular historical situations. But of "concrete laws", substantial uniformities of "economic behaviour", not one—all the really interesting applications of modern statistical technique to economic enquiry have been carried through, not by the Institutionalists, but by men who have been themselves adept in the intricacies

[1] Richard Jones, *Collected Works*, pp. 21 and 22. The comparison is not altogether fair to Jones, who may have been very well justified in some of his criticisms of the Ricardian system. The true precursor of modern "Quantitative Economics" was Sir Josiah Child, who attempted to prove that the concomitance of low interest rates and great riches was an indication that the latter was the result of the former.

of the "orthodox" theoretical analysis. And, at the end of the hundred years, the greatest slump in history finds them sterile and incapable of helpful comment—their trends gone awry and their dispersions distorted.[1] Meanwhile, a few isolated thinkers, using the despised apparatus of deductive theory, have brought our knowledge of the theory of fluctuations to a point from which the fateful events of the last few years can be explained in general terms, and a complete solution of the riddle of depressions within the next few years does not seem outside the bounds of probability.

4. But what, then, are we to say of the more detailed kind of realistic studies? Having ascertained the persistence of the fact of scarcity, the multiplicity of factors of production, ignorance of the future, and the other qualitative postulates of his theory, is the economist then excused from the obligation of maintaining further contact with reality?

The answer is most decidedly in the negative. And the negative answer is implicit in the practice of all those economists who, since Adam Smith and Cantillon, have contributed most to the development of Economic Science. It has never been the case that the exponents of the so-called orthodox tradition have frowned upon realistic studies. As Menger pointed out years ago, at the height of the *Methodenstreit*,[2] the analytical school have never been the assailants in these controversies. Economics is not one of those

---

[1] The discredit of the Historical School in Germany is very largely due to the failure of its members to understand the currency disturbances of the War and the post-War period. It is not improbable that the utter failure of "Quantitative Economics" to understand or predict the great depression may be followed by a similar revulsion. It would certainly be difficult to imagine a more complete or more conspicuous exposure.

[2] *Die Irrthümer des Historismus*, Preface, pp. iii. and iv.

social sciences which are always discussing method before proceeding to deliver the goods; if it had not been for the Historical School there would have been no methodological controversy save such as related to the status of particular propositions. The procedure of "orthodoxy" has always been essentially catholic. The attacks, the attempts to exclude, have always come from the other side. The analytics have always acknowledged the importance of "realistic" studies, and have themselves contributed much to the development of the technique of investigation. Indeed, it is notorious that the most important work of this kind has come, not from this or that "rebel" group who were calling in question the application in Economics of the elementary laws of thought, but rather from just those men who were the object of their onslaught. In the history of applied Economics, the work of a Jevons, a Menger, a Bowley, has much more claim on our attention than the work of, say, a Schmoller, a Veblen, or a Hamilton. And this is no accident. The fruitful conduct of realistic investigations can only be undertaken by those who have a firm grasp of analytical principle and some notion of what can and what cannot legitimately be expected from activities of this sort.

But what, then, are legitimate expectations in this respect? We may group them under three headings.

The first and the most obvious is the provision of a check on the applicability to given situations of different types of theoretical constructions. As we have seen already, the *validity* of a particular theory is a matter of its logical derivation from the general assumptions which it makes. But its *applicability* to a given situation depends upon the extent to which its concepts actually reflect the forces operating in that situation. Now the concrete manifestations of scarcity are various and changing; and, unless there is continuous check on the words which are used to describe them, there is always a danger that the area of application of a particular principle may be misconceived. The terminology of theory and the terminology of practice, although apparently identical, may, in fact, cover different areas.

A simple illustration will make this clear. According to pure monetary theory, if the quantity of money in circulation is increased and other things remain the same, the value of money must fall. This proposition is deducible from the most elementary facts of experience of the science, and its truth is independent of further inductive test. But its applicability to a given situation depends upon a correct understanding of what things are to be regarded as money; and this is a matter which can only be discovered by reference back to the facts. It may well be that over a period of time the concrete significance of the term "money" has altered. If then, while retaining the original term, we proceed to interpret a new situation in terms of the original content, we may be led into serious misapprehension. We may even conclude that the *theory* is fallacious. It is indeed well known that this has happened again and again in the course of the history of theory. The failure of the Currency School to secure permanent acceptance for their theory of Banking and the Exchanges, in other respects so greatly superior to that of their opponents, was notoriously due to their failure to perceive the importance of including Bank Credit in their conception of money. Only by continuous sifting and scrutiny of the changing body of facts[1] can such misapprehensions be avoided.

Secondly, and closely connected with this first function of realistic studies, we may expect the suggestion of those auxiliary postulates whose part in the structure of analysis was discussed in the last chapter By inspection of different fields of economic activity we may expect to discover types of the configuration of the data suitable for further analytical study.

Again, we may take an example from the theory of money. It will be clear from an inspection of the actual procedure of banks of issue that the effect upon the supply of money in the widest sense of given additions to the reserve of precious metals will depend upon the exact nature of the law and practice concerning reserve requirements. It follows, therefore, that in the full elaboration of the theory of money we must introduce alternative assumptions, taking account of the various possibilities in this respect. It is clear that these are not possibilities which are necessarily easily exhausted by general reflections on the nature of banks of issue. Only close study of the facts is likely to reveal which assumptions are most likely to have a counterpart in reality, which assumptions, therefore, it is most convenient to make.

And, thirdly, we may expect of realistic studies not merely a knowledge of the application of par ticular theories, and the assumptions which make them appropriate to particular situations, but also the exposure of areas where pure theory needs to be reformulated and extended. They bring to light new problems.

[1] Professor Jacob Viner's *Canadian Balance of International Indebtedness* and Professor Taussig's *International Trade* provide classical examples of this kind of investigation.

The best example of the unexplained residue is provided by those fluctuations of trade which have come to be known as the trade cycle. Elementary equilibrium theory, as is well known, does not provide any explanation of the phenomena of booms and slumps. It explains the relationships in an economic system on a state of rest. As we have seen, with a certain extension of its assumptions it can describe differences between the relationships resulting from different configurations of the data. But it does not explain without further elaboration the existence within the economic system of tendencies conducive to disproportionate development. It does not explain discrepancies between total supply and total demand in the sense in which these terms are used in the celebrated Law of Markets.[1] Yet unquestionably such discrepancies exist, and any attempt to interpret reality solely in terms of such a theory must necessarily leave a residue of phenomena not capable of being subsumed under its generalisations.

Here is a clear case where empirical studies bring us face to face with the insufficiencies of certain generalisations. And it is perhaps in the revelation of deficiencies of this kind that the main function of realistic studies in relation to theory consists.[2] The theoretical economist who wishes to safeguard the implications of his theory must be continually "trying out", in the explanation of particular situations, the generalisations he has already achieved. It is in the examination of particular instances that lacunæ in the structure of existing theory tend to be revealed.

[1] On all this see Hayek, *Monetary Theory and the Trade Cycle*, chaps i. and ii., *passim*.

[2] Another important function, this time in relation to practice, will be discussed in the next section.

But this is not in the least to say that the *solutions* of the problems thus presented are themselves to be discovered by the mere multiplication of observations of divergences of this sort. That is not the function of observation, and the whole history of the various "inductive revolts" shows that all studies based on this expectation have proved utterly fruitless. This is particularly true of trade cycle theory. So long as the investigators of this problem were content with the multiplication of time series and the accumulation of coefficients of correlation, no significant advance was discernible. It was not until there arose men who were prepared to undertake the entirely different task of starting where elementary theoretical analysis leaves off and deriving from the introduction of further assumptions of the elementary qualitative nature we have already examined, an explanation of fluctuation which is compatible with the assumptions of that analysis, that progress began to be made. There can be no better example of the correct relationship between the two branches of study. Realistic studies may suggest the problem to be solved. They may test the range of applicability of the answer when it is forthcoming. They may suggest assumptions for further theoretical elaboration. But it is theory and theory alone which is capable of supplying the solution. Any attempt to reverse the relationship must lead inevitably to the nirvana of purposeless observation and record.

Moreover—and this brings us back to the point from which we started—there is no reason to believe that the generalisations which may be elaborated to explain the residues thus discovered will be anything but general in character. For reasons which we have already examined, the hope of giving permanent and particular content to the categories of pure analysis is vain. By "trying out" pure theory on concrete situations and referring back to pure theory residual difficulties, we may hope continually to improve and extend our analytical apparatus. But that such studies should enable us to say what goods must be economic goods and what precise values will be attached to them in different situations, is not to be expected. To say this is not to abandon the hope of solving any genuine problem of Economics. It is merely to recognise what does and what does not lie within the necessary boundaries of our subject-matter. To pretend that this is not so is just pseudo-scientific bravado.

5. But to recognise that Economic laws are general in nature is not to deny the reality of the necessities they describe or to derogate from their value as a means of interpretation and prediction. On the contrary, having carefully delimited the nature and the scope of such generalisations, we may proceed with all the greater confidence to claim for them a complete necessity within this field.

Economic laws describe inevitable implications. If the data they postulate are given, then the consequences they predict necessarily follow. In this sense they are on the same footing as other scientific laws, and as little capable of "suspension". If, in a given situation, the facts are of a certain order, we are warranted in deducing with complete certainty that other facts which it enables us to describe are also present. To those who have grasped the implications of the propositions set forth in the last chapter the reason is not far to seek. If the "given situation" conforms to a certain pattern, certain other features must also be present, for their presence is "deducible" from the pattern originally postulated. The analytic method is simply a way of discovering the necessary consequences of complex collocations of facts—consequences whose counterpart in reality is not so immediately discernible as the counterpart of the original postulates. It is an instrument for "shaking out" all the implications of given suppositions. Granted the correspondence of its original assumptions and the facts, its conclusions are inevitable and inescapable.

All this becomes particularly clear if we consider the procedure of diagrammatic analysis. Suppose, for example, we wish to exhibit the effects on price of the imposition of a small tax. We make certain suppositions as regards the elasticity of demand, certain suppositions as regards the cost functions, embody these in the usual diagram, and we can at once *read off*, as it were, the effects on the price.[1] They are implied in the original suppositions. The diagram has simply made explicit the concealed implications.

It is this inevitability of economic analysis which gives it its very considerable prognostic value. It has been emphasised sufficiently already that Economic Science knows no way of predicting out of the blue the configuration of the data at any particular point of time. It cannot predict changes of valuations. But, given the data in a particular situation, it can draw inevitable conclusions as to their implications. And if the data remain unchanged, these implications will certainly be realised. They must be, for they are implied in the presence of the original data.

---

[1] See, *e.g.*, Dalton, *Public Finance*, 2nd edition, p. 73.

It is just here that we can perceive yet a further function for empirical investigation. It can bring to light the changing facts which make prediction in any given situation possible. As we have seen, it is most improbable that it can ever discover the law of their change, for the data are not subject to homogeneous causal influences. But it can put us in possession of information which is relevant at the particular moment concerned. It can give us some idea of the relative magnitude of the different forces operative. It can afford a basis for enlightened conjectures with regard to potential directions of change. And this unquestionably is one of the main uses of applied studies—not to unearth "empirical" laws in an area where such laws are not to be expected, but to provide from moment to moment some knowledge of the varying data on which, in the given situation, prediction can be based. It cannot supersede formal analysis. But it can suggest in different situations what formal analysis is appropriate, and it can provide *at that moment* some content for the formal categories.

Of course, if other things do not remain unchanged, the consequences predicted do not necessarily follow. This elementary platitude, necessarily implicit in *any* scientific prediction, needs especially to be kept in the foreground of attention when discussing this kind of prognosis. The statesman who said "*Ceteris paribus* be damned!" has a large and enthusiastic following among the critics of Economics! Nobody in his senses would hold that the laws of mechanics were invalidated if an experiment designed to illustrate them were interrupted by an earthquake. Yet a substantial majority of the lay public, and a good many *soi-disant* economists as well, are continually criticising well-established propositions on grounds hardly less slender.[1] A protective tariff is imposed on the importation of commodities, the conditions of whose domestic production make it certain that, if other things remain unchanged, the effect of such protection will be a rise in price. For quite adventitious reasons, the progress of technique, the lowering of the price of raw materials, wage reductions, or what not, costs are reduced and the price does not rise. In the eyes of the lay public and "Institutionalist" economists the generalisations of Economics are invalidated. The laws of supply and demand are suspended. The bogus claims of a science which does not regard the facts are laid bare. And so on and so forth. Yet, whoever asked of the practitioners of any other

---

[1] See, e.g., the various statistical "refutations" of the quantity theory of money which have appeared in recent years. On all these the comment of Torrens on Tooke is all that need be said. "The History of Prices may be regarded as a psychological study. Mr. Tooke commenced his labours as a follower of Horner and Ricardo, and derived reflected lustre from an alliance with those celebrated names; but his capacity for collecting contemporaneous facts preponderating over his perceptive and logical faculties, his accumulation of facts involved him in a labyrinth of error. Failing to perceive that a theoretical principle, although it may irresistibly command assent under all circumstances coinciding with the premises from which it is deduced, must be applied with due limitation and correction in all cases not coinciding with the premises, he fell into a total misconception of the proposition advanced by Adam Smith, and imputed to that high authority the absurdity of maintaining that variations in the quantity of money cause the money values of all commodities to vary in equal proportions, while the values of commodities, in relation to each other, are varying in unequal proportions. Reasonings derived from this extraordinary misconception necessarily led to extraordinary conclusions. Having satisfied himself that Adam Smith had correctly established as a principle universally true that variations in the purchasing power of money cause the prices of all commodities to vary in equal proportions, and finding, as he pursued his investigations into the phenomena of the market at different periods, no instances in which an expansion or contraction of the circulation caused the prices of commodities to rise or fall in an equal ratio, he arrived by a strictly logical inference from the premises thus illogically assumed, at his grand discovery—that no increase of the circulating medium can have the effect of increasing prices" (*The Principles and Operation of Sir Robert Peel's Act of 1844 Explained and Defended*, 1st edition, p. 75).

science that they should predict the complete course of an uncontrolled history?

Now, no doubt, the very fact that events in the large are uncontrolled,[1] that the fringe of given data is so extensive and so exposed to influence from unexpected quarters, must make the task of prediction, however carefully safeguarded, extremely hazardous. In many situations, small changes in particular groups of data are so liable to be counterbalanced by other changes which may be occurring independently and simultaneously, that the prognostic value of the knowledge of operative tendencies is small. But there are certain broad changes, usually involving many lines of expenditure or production at once, where a knowledge of implications is a very firm basis for conjectures of strong probability. This is particularly the case in the sphere of monetary phenomena. There can be no question that a quite elementary knowledge of the Quantity Theory was of immense prognostic value during the War and the disturbances which followed. If the speculators who bought German marks, after the War, in the confident expectation that the mark would automatically resume its old value, had been aware of as much of the theory of money as was known, say, to Sir William Petty, they would have known that what they were doing was

[1] The alleged advantage of economic "planning"—namely, that it enables greater certainty with regard to the future—depends upon the assumption that under "planning" the present controlling forces, the choices of individual spenders and savers, are themselves brought under the control of the planners. The paradox therefore arises that either the planner is destitute of the instrument of calculating the ends of the community he intends to serve, or, if he restores the instrument, he removes the *raison d'être* of the "plan". Of course, the dilemma does not arise if he thinks himself capable of interpreting these ends or—what is much more probable—if he has no intention of serving any other ends but those *he* thinks appropriate. Strange to say this not infrequently happens. Scratch a would-be planner and you usually find a would-be dictator.

ridiculous. Similarly, it becomes more and more
clear, for purely analytical reasons, that, once the
signs of a major boom in trade have made their
appearance, the coming of slump and depression is
almost certain; though when it will come and how long
it will last are not matters which are predictable,
since they depend upon human volitions occurring
after the indications in question have appeared. So,
too, in the sphere of the labour market, it is quite
certain that some types of wage policy must result
in unemployment if other things remain equal: and
knowledge of how the "other things" must change
in order that this consequence may be avoided makes
it very often possible to predict with considerable
confidence the actual results of given policies. These
things have been verified again and again in practice.
Today it is only he who is blind because he does not
want to see who is prepared to deny them. If certain
conditions are present, then, in the absence of new
complications, certain consequences are inevitable.

6. None the less, economic laws have their limits,
and, if we are to use them wisely, it is important that
we should realise exactly wherein these limitations
consist. In the light of what has been said already,
this should not be difficult.

The irrational element in the economist's universe
of discourse lies behind the individual valuation. As
we have seen already, there is no means available for
determining the probable movement of the relative
scales of valuation.[1] Hence in all our analysis we take

---

[1] It should be observed that this is not the same as saying that there is
no means available for defining the probable movement of the demand curve.
It is important to realise that the demand curve is to be conceived as derived
from the more fundamental indifference system, and it is to this latter that
our proposition relates.

the scales of valuation as given. It is only what follows
from these given assumptions that has the character
of inevitability. It is only in this area that we find the
régime of law.

It follows, therefore, that economic laws cannot
be held to relate to movements of the relative scales,
and that economic causation only extends through the
range of their original implication. This is not to say
that changes in values may not be contemplated.
Of course, changes in values are the main preoccupation of theoretical Economics. It is only to say that,
as economists, we cannot go behind changes in
individual valuations. We may explain, in terms
of economic law, relationships which follow from
given technical conditions and relative valuations.
We may explain changes due to changes in these
data. But we cannot explain changes in the data
themselves. To demarcate these types of change
the Austrians[1] distinguish between endogenous and
exogenous changes. The ones occur within a given
structure of assumptions. The others come from
outside.

We can see the relevance of these distinctions to
the problem of prognosis if we consider once more the
implications of the theory of money. Given certain
assumptions with regard to the demand for money,
we are justified in asserting that an increase in the
volume of any currency will be followed by a fall in
its external value. This is an endogenous change. It
follows from the original assumptions, and, so long as
they hold, it is clearly inevitable. We are not justified
in asserting. however, as has been so often asserted

---

[1] See especially Strigl, *Aenderungen in den Daten der Wirtschaft (Jahr-
bücher für Nationalökonomie und Statistik*, vol. cxxviii., pp. 641-662).

in recent years, that if the exchanges fall, inflation *must* necessarily follow. We know that very often this happens. We know that governments are often foolish and craven and that false views of the functions of money are widely prevalent. But there is no *inevitable* connection between a fall in the exchanges and a decision to set the printing presses working. A new human volition interrupts the chain of "causation". But between the issue of paper money and the fall in its external value, no change in the assumed disposition to action on the part of the various economic subjects concerned is contemplated. All that happens is, as it were, that the exchange index moves to a lower level.

A more complicated example of the same distinction is provided by the Reparations controversy. Suppose that it could be shown that the external demand for German products was very inelastic, so that in the short period, at any rate, the degree of necessary transfer burden over and above the burden of paying the domestic taxes was very great. In such circumstances it might be argued that the present crisis was directly due to purely economic factors. That is to say that, up to the point at which panic supervened, the various complications were entirely due to obstacles implicit in the given conditions of world supply and demand.[1] But suppose it can be shown that the prime cause of the present difficulty was financial panic, induced by the fear of political revolt at the magnitude of the original tax burden, then it cannot be argued that the train of causation was wholly economic. The political reaction to the

[1] This is the limiting case discussed in Dr. Machlup's *Transfer und Preisbewegung* (*Zeitschrift für Nationalökonomie*, vol. i., pp. 555-561).

tax burden intervenes. The "transfer crisis" arises from exogenous causes.[1]

Now there can be no doubt that this distinction is not always easy to draw. In some cases there may be a functional connection between rates of remuneration and increments of the quantity and the quality of the working population. How is this to be regarded? So far as the response is concerned, it is endogenous. But so far as the configuration of the market demand is concerned, it is exogenous. New people with new scales of relative valuation appear. Again, as Professor Knight has often pointed out, the situation is further complicated by the fact that in some societies there exist definite financial incentives to certain individuals to produce changes in the data. Resources are devoted to changing technical knowledge by research, and the tastes of economic subjects by persuasion. In respect of such changes the distinction is difficult to apply. We must admit that the system is "open". Nevertheless, over a large part of the field the classification is intelligible enough and a positive aid to clear thinking. Until matters have been clarified very much further its retention seems essential.

---

[1] Professor Souter says that words fail him to describe the type of mind that takes any pleasure in drawing such distinctions (*op. cit.*, p. 139). But surely, methodological considerations apart, there are very solid reasons of convenience for observing them. I venture to suggest that if Professor Souter had been asked to advise any Government on such questions there would have come a point at which, having diagnosed the "economic" factors, he would have turned and said, "But then, of course, there is the political problem; will people stand it?" And he might have added with Cantillon, "But that is not my business". Or, as true blue Hegelian, taking all knowledge for his province, he might have then launched forth on a disquisition of what is and what is not politically possible. But he would have made the distinction. Exactly how he labelled it we might argue about in a friendly way afterwards.

In the same way it should be recognised that in the discussion of practical problems, certain kinds of exogenous changes, apparently closely connected with changes within the chain of economic causation, are not infrequently involved. In the sphere of monetary problems the danger that falling exchanges may induce the monetary authorities of the area involved to embark on inflation, will certainly be considered germane to the discussion. In the sphere of tariff policy, the tendency of the granting of a protective tariff to create monopolistic communities of interest among domestic producers is certainly a probability which should not be overlooked by the practical administrator. Here and in many other connections there is a penumbra of psychological probabilities which, for purely practical reasons, it is often very convenient to take into account.[1] No doubt the kind of insight required into these problems is often of a very elementary order—although it is surprising how many people lack it. No doubt most of the probabilities involved are virtual certainties. Men in possession of their senses are not likely to question them as working maxims of political practice. Still, not all

---

[1] I venture, as in the first edition, to draw attention to the actual words used in this prescription. It is more accuracy in mode of statement, not over-austerity in speculative range, for which I am pleading. I am very far from suggesting that, when discussing practical problems, economists should refrain from contemplating the probability of those changes in the data whose causation falls outside the strict limits of Economic Science. Indeed, I am inclined to believe that there is here a field of sociological speculation in which economists may have a definite advantage over others. Certainly it is a field in which hitherto they have done very much more than others—one has only to think of the various discussions of the possible forms of a Tariff Commission in a democratic community or the necessary conditions of bureaucratic administration of productive enterprise to see the sort of thing I have in mind. All that I am contending is the desirability of recognising the distinction between the kind of generalisation which belongs to this field and the kind which belongs to Economics proper.

participants in discussions of this sort are in possession of their senses, and while it is highly desirable that the economist who wishes that the applications of his science should be fruitful should be fully qualified in cognate disciplines, and should be prepared to invoke their assistance, it is also highly desirable that the distinction should be recognised between those generalisations which are economic in the sense in which the word has here been used, and those generalisations of the "sociological penumbra" which do not have the same degree of probability. Economists have nothing to lose by understating rather than overstating the extent of their certainty. Indeed, it is only when this is done that the overwhelming power to convince of what remains can be expected to have free play.

7. All this has a very intimate bearing on the question which we left unanswered at the end of the last chapter. Is it not possible for us to extend our generalisations so as to cover changes of the data? We have seen in what sense it is possible to conceive of economic dynamics—the analysis of the path through time of a system making adjustments consequential upon the existence of given conditions? Can we not extend our technique so as to enable us to predict changes of these given conditions? In short, can we not frame a complete theory of economic development?

If the preceding analysis is correct the prospects are very doubtful. If we were able to ascertain once and for all the elasticities of demand for all possible commodities and the elasticities of supply of all factors, and if we could assume that these coefficients were constant, then we might indeed conceive of a grand calculation which would enable an economic Laplace to foretell the economic appearance of our universe at any moment in the future. But, as we have seen, useful as such calculations are for judging the immediate potentialities of particular situations, there is no reason for attributing to them permanent validity. Our economic Laplace must fail in that there are no constants of this sort in his system. We have, as it were, to rediscover our various laws of gravitation from moment to moment.

But is it not possible in a more formal sense to predict broad changes of the data? We may not be able to foretell particular tastes and the relationships between particular commodities, but by including in our conception of endogenous change, changes such as those indicated above, responses of the population to changes in income, induced invention, and so on, can we not still provide a formal outline of probable developments which shall be useful?

Now there is no doubt that so far as population change is concerned it is possible to conceive of movements as responsive to money incentives. We can conceive, as did the classical economists, of a final equilibrium in which the value of the discounted future remuneration of labour is equal to the discounted costs of bearing, rearing, and training labourers. It is doubtful whether it is very profitable to assume this particular functional connection in dealing with societies other than communities of slave owners. For, save in this case, it must be remembered that we are not entitled to assume, as did the classical economists at one stage, that the costs which are equated to the gains are objective in character: the equilibrium rate outside the slave society is that which will *induce* the constant supply of labourers, not merely that which makes it *physiologically possible* to support them. Still, for what it is worth, such an assumption can be made.

But even so we have only described in formal terms a condition of final equilibrium. We have done nothing which enables us to predict *changes* in the ultimate conditions of supply of labourers. The broad vicissitudes of opinion on the optional size of family or the most desirable entourage of slaves—these lie outside the scope of our technique of prediction. Who is to say whether the present influences on the size of the family, which bid fair, if they continue for a few millennia, to reduce the population of Europe to a few hundred thousands of people, will persist, or whether they will give way before the onset of new faiths, new conceptions of duty, new conceptions of the essentials of a good life? We may all venture our guess. But surely economic analysis can have very little to do with it.

Nor are the prospects improved when we turn to the sphere of technical change and invention. As Professor Schumpeter has emphasised, it is very difficult to conceive even of equilibrium adjustments here. Perhaps with some ingenuity it could be done. But how would that help us to predict—what would be necessary for a theory of development in the sense in which we are now using the word—the *nature* of the changes forthcoming? What technique of analysis could predict the trends of inventions leading on the one hand to the coming of the railway, on the other to the internal combustion engine. Even if we think that, if we know the technique, we can predict the type of economic relationship associated with it, which of course is highly disputable, how can we predict the

technique? As the examples just quoted amply illustrate, it is not at all true that the trend is all in one
direction. We need postulate no ultimate indeterminism, if we assume that, from the point of view of
our system, such changes are unpredictable.

So, too, when we turn to the question of changes in
the legal framework within which we conceive the
adjustments we study to operate. There is an important sense in which the subject-matter of political
science can be conceived to come within the scope of
our definition of the economic. Systems of government, property relationships, and the like, can be
conceived as the result of choice. It is desirable that
this conception should be further explored on lines
analogous to better known analysis. But how can we
tell in advance what choice will be made? How can
we predict the substance of the political indifference
systems?

It is well known that the claim has been made to
interpret the evolution of political forms in terms of
the distribution of "economic" power and the play of
"economic" interest. And it would be foolish to deny
that, within limits, elucidations of this sort can be
provided which are at least intelligible. But on closer
examination the limits within which this sort of thing
is possible are seen to be much narrower than is often
believed to be the case. We may perhaps explain
particular political changes in terms of the "interest"
of particular groups of producers; the machinery of
the market affords at least a loose and superficial
index of short period interest which is capable of objective definition. But the plausibility of the more
grandiose explanations of this kind rest upon the assumption that the interests of larger groups are equally

capable of objective definition. And this is not true.
So far from providing a justification for this kind
of economic explanation, economic analysis suggests
that it is definitely false. The concept of interest involved in all these explanations is not objective, but
subjective. It is a function of what people believe and
feel. And there is no technique in economics which
enables us to forecast these permutations of the spirit.
We may forecast their effects when they have occurred.
We may speculate with regard to the effects of hypothetical changes. We may consider alternative forms
and enquire concerning their stability and tendency to
change. But as regards our actual capacity to foretell a
process of change, with its manifest dependence on the
heterogeneous elements of contingency, persuasion, and
blind force, if we are humble, we shall be modest in our
pretensions.

Thus in the last analysis the study of Economics,
while it shows us a region of economic laws, of necessities to which human action is subject, shows us, too,
a region in which no such necessities operate. This is
not to say that within that region there is no law, no
necessity. Into that question we make no enquiry. It
is only to say that from its point of view at least there
are certain things which must be taken as ultimate
data.

CHAPTER VI

THE SIGNIFICANCE OF ECONOMIC SCIENCE

1. WE now approach the last stage of our investigations. We have surveyed the subject-matter of Economics. We have examined the nature of its generalisations and their bearing on the interpretation of reality. We have finally to ask: What is the significance of it all for social life and conduct ? What is the bearing of Economic Science on practice?

2. It is sometimes thought that certain developments in modern Economic Theory furnish *by themselves* a set of norms capable of providing a basis for political practice. The Law of Diminishing Marginal Utility is held to provide a criterion of all forms of political and social activity affecting distribution. Anything conducive to greater equality, which does not adversely affect production, is said to be justified by this law; anything conducive to inequality, condemned. These propositions have received the support of very high authority. They are the basis of much that is written on the theory of public finance.[1] No less an authority than Professor Cannan has invoked them, to justify the ways of economists to Fabian Socialists.[2] They have received the widest countenance in number-

---

[1] See, *e.g.*, Edgeworth, *The Pure Theory of Taxation* (*Papers Relating to Political Economy*, vol. ii., p. 63 *seq.*).

[2] See *Economics and Socialism* (*The Economic Outlook*, pp. 59-62).

less works on Applied Economics. It is safe to say that the great majority of English economists accept them as axiomatic. Yet with great diffidence I venture to suggest that they are in fact entirely unwarranted by any doctrine of scientific economics, and that outside this country they have very largely ceased to hold sway.

The argument by which these propositions are supported is familiar: but it is worth while repeating it explicitly in order to show the exact points at which it is defective. The Law of Diminishing Marginal Utility implies that the more one has of anything the less one values additional units thereof. Therefore, it is said, the more real income one has, the less one values additional units of income. Therefore the marginal utility of a rich man's income is less than the marginal utility of a poor man's income. Therefore, if transfers are made, and these transfers do not appreciably affect production, total utility will be increased. Therefore, such transfers are "economically justified". *Quod erat demonstrandum.*

At first sight the plausibility of the argument is overwhelming. But on closer inspection it is seen to be merely specious. It rests upon an extension of the conception of diminishing marginal utility into a field in which it is entirely illegitimate. The "Law of Diminishing Marginal Utility" here invoked does not follow in the least from the fundamental conception of economic goods; and it makes assumptions which, whether they are true or false, can never be verified by observation or introspection. The proposition we are examining begs the great metaphysical question of the scientific comparability of different individual experiences. This deserves further examination.

The Law of Diminishing Marginal Utility, as we

have seen, is derived from the conception of a scarcity
of means in relation to the ends which they serve. It
assumes that, for each individual, goods can be ranged
in order of their significance for conduct; and that, in
the sense that it will be preferred, we can say that one
use of a good is more important than another. Proceeding on this basis, we can compare the order in which
one individual may be supposed to prefer certain
alternatives with the order in which they are preferred by another individual. In this way it is possible
to build up a complete theory of exchange.[1]

But it is one thing to assume that scales can be
drawn up showing the *order* in which an individual
will prefer a series of alternatives, and to compare the
arrangement of one such individual scale with another.
It is quite a different thing to assume that behind such
arrangements lie magnitudes which themselves can be
compared. This is not an assumption which need anywhere be made in modern economic analysis, and it
is an assumption which is of an entirely different
kind from the assumption of individual scales of relative valuation. The theory of exchange assumes that
I can compare the importance *to me* of bread at 6d.
per loaf and 6d. spent on other alternatives presented
by the opportunities of the market. And it assumes
that the order of my preferences thus exhibited can
be compared with the order of preferences of the
baker. But it does *not* assume that, at any point, it
is necessary to compare the satisfaction which *I* get
from the spending of 6d. on bread with the satis-

---

1 So many have been the misconceptions based upon an imperfect understanding of this generalisation that Dr. Hicks has suggested that its present
name be discarded altogether and the title Law of Increasing Rate of Sub-
stitution be adopted in its place. Personally, I prefer the established
terminology, but it is clear that there is much to be said for the suggestion.

faction which *the Baker* gets by receiving it. That comparison is a comparison of an entirely different nature. It is a comparison which is never needed in the theory of equilibrium and which is never implied by the assumptions of that theory. It is a comparison which necessarily falls outside the scope of any positive science. To state that A's preference stands above B's in order of importance is entirely different from stating that A prefers *n* to *m* and B prefers *n* and *m* in a different order. It involves an element of conventional valuation. Hence it is essentially normative. It has no place in pure science.

If this is still obscure, the following considerations should be decisive. Suppose that a difference of opinion were to arise about A's preferences. Suppose that I thought that, at certain prices, he preferred *n* to *m*, and you thought that, at the same prices, he preferred *m* to *n*. It would be easy to settle our differences in a purely scientific manner. Either we could ask A to tell us. Or, if we refused to believe that introspection on A's part was possible, we could expose him to the stimuli in question and observe his behaviour. Either test would be such as to provide the basis for a settlement of the difference of opinion.

But suppose that we differed about the satisfaction derived by A from an income of £1,000, and the satisfaction derived by B from an income of twice that magnitude. Asking them would provide no solution. Supposing they differed. A might urge that he had more satisfaction than B at the margin. While B might urge that, on the contrary, he had more satisfaction than A. We do not need to be slavish behaviourists to realise that here is no scientific evidence. *There is no means of testing the magnitude of*

A's satisfaction as compared with B's. If we tested the state of their blood-streams, that would be a test of blood, not satisfaction. Introspection does not enable A to measure what is going on in B's mind, nor B to measure what is going on in A's. There is no way of comparing the satisfactions of different people.

Now, of course, in daily life we do continually assume that the comparison can be made. But the very diversity of the assumptions actually made at different times and in different places is evidence of their conventional nature. In Western democracies we assume for certain purposes that men in similar circumstances are capable of equal satisfactions. Just as for purposes of justice we assume equality of responsibility in similar situations as between legal subjects, so for purposes of public finance we agree to assume equality of capacity for experiencing satisfaction from equal incomes in similar circumstances as between economic subjects. But, although it may be convenient to assume this, there is no way of proving that the assumption rests on ascertainable fact. And, indeed, if the representative of some other civilisation were to assure us that we were wrong, that members of his caste (or his race) were capable of experiencing ten times as much satisfaction from given incomes as members of an inferior caste (or an "inferior" race), we could not refute him. We might poke fun at him. We might flare up with indignation, and say that his valuation was hateful, that it led to civil strife, unhappiness, unjust privilege, and so on and so forth. But we could not show that he was wrong in any objective sense, any more than we could show that we were right. And since in our hearts we do not regar l different men's satisfactions from similar means as equally valuable, it would really be rather silly if we continued to pretend that the justification for our scheme of things was in any way *scientific*. It can be justified on grounds of general convenience. Or it can be justified by appeal to ultimate standards of obligation. But it cannot be justified by appeal to any kind of positive science.

Hence the extension of the Law of Diminishing Marginal Utility, postulated in the propositions we are examining, is illegitimate. And the arguments based upon it therefore are lacking in scientific foundation. Recognition of this no doubt involves a substantial curtailment of the claims of much of what now assumes the status of scientific generalisation in current discussions of applied Economics. The conception of diminishing relative utility (the convexity downwards of the indifference curve) does not justify the inference that transferences from the rich to the poor will increase total satisfaction. It does not tell us that a graduated income tax is less injurious to the social dividend than a non-graduated poll tax. Indeed, all that part of the theory of public finance which deals with "Social Utility" must assume a different significance. Interesting as a development of an ethical postulate, it does not at all follow from the positive assumptions of pure theory. It is simply the accidental deposit of the historical association of English Economics with Utilitarianism: and both the utilitarian postulates from which it derives and the analytical Economics with which it has been associated will be the better and the more convincing if this is clearly recognised.[1]

---

[1] Cp. Davenport, *Value and Distribution*, pp. 301 and 571; Benham, *Economic Welfare* (*Economica*, June, 1930, pp. 173-187); M. St. Braun,

But supposing this were not so. Suppose that we could bring ourselves to believe in the positive status of these conventional assumptions, the commensurability of different experiences, the equality of capacity for satisfaction, etc. And suppose that, proceeding on this basis, we had succeeded in showing that certain policies *had the effect* of increasing "social utility", even so it would be totally illegitimate to argue that such a conclusion by itself warranted the inference that these policies *ought* to be carried out. For such an inference would beg the whole question whether the increase of satisfaction in this sense was socially obligatory.[1] And there is nothing within the body of economic generalisations, even thus enlarged by the inclusion of elements of conventional valuation, which affords any means of deciding this question. Propositions involving "ought" are on an entirely

---

Theorie der staatlichen Wirtschaftspolitik, pp. 41-44. Even Professor Irving Fisher, anxious to provide a justification for his statistical method for measuring "marginal utility", can find no better apology for his procedure than that "Philosophic doubt is right and proper, but the problems of life cannot and do not wait" (*Economic Essays in Honour of John Bates Clark*, p. 180). It does not seem to me that the problem of measuring marginal utility as between individuals is a particularly pressing problem. But whether this is so or not, the fact remains that Professor Fisher solves his problem only by making a conventional assumption. And it does not seem that it anywhere aids the solution of practical problems to pretend that conventional assumptions have scientific justification. It does not make me a more docile democrat to be told that *I* am equally capable of experiencing satisfaction as my neighbour; it fills me with indignation. But I am perfectly willing to accept the statement that it is *convenient* to assume that this is the case. I am quite willing to accept the argument—indeed, as distinct from believers in the racial or proletarian myths, I very firmly believe —that, in modern conditions, societies which proceed on any other assumption have an inherent instability. But we are past the days when democracy could be made acceptable by the pretence that judgments of value are judgments of scientific fact. I am afraid that the same strictures apply to the highly ingenious *Methods for Measuring Marginal Utility* of Professor Ragnar Frisch.

[1] Psychological hedonism in so far as it went beyond the individual may have involved a non-scientific assumption, but it was not by itself a necessary justification for ethical hedonism.

different plane from propositions involving "is". But more of this later.[1]

3. Exactly the same type of stricture may be applied to any attempt to make the criteria of free equilibrium in the price system at the same time the criteria of "economic justification". The pure theory of equilibrium enables us to understand how, given the valuations of the various economic subjects and the facts of the legal and technical environment, a system of relationships can be conceived from which there would be no tendency to variation. It enables us to describe that distribution of resources which, given the valuations of the individual concerned, satisfies demand most fully. But it does not by itself provide any ethical sanctions. To show that, under certain conditions, demand is satisfied more adequately than under any alternative set of conditions, does not prove that that set of conditions is desirable. There is no penumbra of approbation round the theory of equilibrium. Equilibrium is just equilibrium.

Now, of course, it is of the essence of the conception of equilibrium that, given his initial resources, each individual secures a range of free choice, bounded only by the limitations of the material environment and the exercise of a similar freedom on the part of the other economic subjects. In equilibrium each individual is free to move to a different point on his lines of preference, but he does not move, for, in the circumstances postulated, any other point would be less preferred. Given certain norms of political philosophy, this conception may throw an important light upon the types of social institutions necessary to

[1] See below, Section 4.

achieve them.[1] But freedom to choose may not be regarded as an ultimate good. The creation of a state of affairs offering the maximum freedom of choice may not be thought desirable, having regard to other social ends. To show that, in certain conditions, the maximum of freedom of this sort is achieved is not to show that those conditions should be sought after.

Moreover, there are certain obvious limitations on the possibility of formulating ends in price offers. To secure the conditions within which the equilibrating tendencies may emerge there must exist a certain legal apparatus, not capable of being elicited by price bids, yet essential for their orderly execution.[2] The negative condition of health, immunity from infectious disease, is not an end which can be wholly achieved by individual action. In urban conditions the failure of one individual to conform to certain sanitary requirements may involve all the others in an epidemic. The securing of ends of this sort must necessarily involve the using of factors of production in a way not fully compatible with complete freedom in the expenditure of given individual resources. And it is clear that society, acting as a body of political citizens, may formulate ends which interfere much more drastically than this with the free choices of the individuals composing it. There is nothing in the corpus of economic analysis which in itself affords any justification for regarding these ends as good or bad. Economic analysis can

[1] See two very important papers by Professor Plant, *Co-ordination and Competition in Transport* (*Journal of the Institute of Transport*, vol. xiii., pp. 127-136); *Trends in Business Administration* (*Economica*, No. 35, pp. 45-62).

[2] On the place of the legal framework of Economic Activity, the "organisation" of the Economy as he calls it, Dr. Strigl's work cited above is very illuminating. See Strigl, *op. cit.,* pp. 85-121.

simply point out the implications as regards the disposal of means of production of the various patterns of ends which may be chosen.

For this reason, the use of the adjectives "economical" and "uneconomical" to describe certain policies is apt to be very misleading. The criterion of economy which follows from our original definitions is the securing of given ends with least means. It is, therefore, perfectly intelligible to say of a certain policy that it is uneconomical, if, in order to achieve certain ends, it uses more scarce means than are necessary. Once the ends by which they are valued are given as regards the disposition of means, the terms "economical " and "uneconomical" can be used with complete intelligibility.

But it is not intelligible to use them as regards ends themselves. As we have seen already, there are no economic ends.[1] There are only economical and uneconomical ways of achieving given ends. We cannot say that the pursuit of given ends is uneconomical because the ends are uneconomical; we can only say it is uneconomical if the ends are pursued with an unnecessary expenditure of means.

Thus it is not legitimate to say that going to war is uneconomical, if, having regard to all the issues and all the sacrifices necessarily involved, it is decided that the anticipated result is worth the sacrifice. It is only legitimate so to describe it if it is attempted to secure this end with an unnecessary degree of sacrifice.

It is the same with measures more specifically "economic"—to use the term in its confused popular sense. If we assume that the ends of public policy are

---

[1] See Chapter II., Sections 2 and 3, above.

the safeguarding of conditions under which individual demands, as reflected in the price system, are satisfied as amply as possible under given conditions, then, save in very special circumstances which are certainly not generally known to those who impose such measures, it is legitimate to say that a protective tariff on wheat is uneconomical in that it imposes obstacles to the achievement of this end. This follows clearly from purely neutral analysis. But if the object in view transcends these ends—if the tariff is designed to bring about an end not formulated in consumers' price offers—the safeguarding of food supply against the danger of war, for instance—it is not legitimate to say that it is uneconomical just because it results in the impoverishment of consumers. In such circumstances the only justification for describing it as uneconomical would be a demonstration that it achieved this end also with an unnecessary sacrifice of means.[1]

Again, we may examine the case of minimum wage regulation. It is a well-known generalisation of theoretical Economics that a wage which is held above the equilibrium level necessarily involves unemployment and a diminution of the value of capital. This is one of the most elementary deductions from the theory of economic equilibrium. The history of this country since the War is one long vindication of its accuracy.[2] The popular view that the validity of these "static" deductions is vitiated by the probability of "dynamic improvements" induced by wage pressure, depends upon an oversight of the fact that these "improve-

[1] See a paper by the present author on *The Case of Agriculture* in *Tariffs: The Case Examined* (edited by Sir William Beveridge).

[2] Hicks, *The Theory of Wages*, chs. ix and x. On the evidence of post-War history, Dr. Benham's *Wages, Prices and Unemployment* (*Economist*, June 20, 1931) should be consulted.

ments" are themselves one of the manifestations of capital wastage.[1] But such a policy is not *necessarily* to be described as uneconomical. If, in the society imposing such a policy, it is generally thought that the gain of the absence of wage payments below a certain rate more than compensates for the unemployment and losses it involves, the policy cannot be described as uneconomical. As private individuals we may think that such a system of preferences sacrifices tangible increments of the ingredients of real happiness for the false end of a mere diminution of inequality. We may suspect that those who cherish such preferences are deficient in imagination. But there is nothing in scientific Economics which warrants us in passing these judgments. Economics is neutral as between ends. Economics cannot pronounce on the validity of ultimate judgments of value.

4. In recent years, certain economists, realising this inability of Economics, thus conceived, to provide within itself a series of principles binding upon practice, have urged that the boundaries of the subject should be extended to include normative studies. Mr. Hawtrey and Mr. J. A. Hobson, for instance, have argued that Economics should not only take account of valuations and ethical standards as given data in the manner explained above, but that also it should pronounce upon the ultimate validity of these valuations and standards.

---

[1] It is curious that this should not have been more generally realised, for it is usually the most enthusiastic exponents of this view who also denounce most vigorously the unemployment "caused" by rationalisation. It is, of course, the necessity of the conversion of capital into forms which are profitable at the higher wage level which is responsible both for a shrinkage in social capital and the creation of an industrial structure incapable of affording full employment to the whole working population. There is no reason to expect permanent unemployment as a result of rationalisation *not* induced by wages above the equilibrium level.

"Economics", says Mr. Hawtrey, "cannot be dissociated from Ethics".[1]

Unfortunately it does not seem logically possible to associate the two studies in any form but mere juxtaposition. Economics deals with ascertainable facts; ethics with valuations and obligations. The two fields of enquiry are not on the same plane of discourse. Between the generalisations of positive and normative studies there is a logical gulf fixed which no ingenuity can disguise and no juxtaposition in space or time bridge over. The proposition that the price of pork fluctuates with variations in supply and demand follows from a conception of the relation of pork to human impulses which, in the last resort, is verifiable by introspection and observation. We can ask people whether they are prepared to buy pork and how much they are prepared to buy at different prices. Or we can watch how they behave when equipped with currency and exposed to the stimuli of the pig-meat markets.[2] But the proposition that it is *wrong* that pork should be valued, although it is a proposition which has greatly influenced the conduct of different races,

---

[1] See Hawtrey, *The Economic Problem*, especially pp. 184 and 203-215, and Hobson, *Wealth and Life*, pp. 112-140. I have examined Mr. Hawtrey's contentions in some detail in an article entitled, *Mr. Hawtrey on the Scope of Economics* (*Economica*, No. 20, pp. 172-178). But in that article I made certain statements with regard to the claims of "welfare Economics" which I should now wish to formulate rather differently. Moreover, at that time I did not understand the nature of the idea of *precision* in economic generalisations, and my argument contains one entirely unnecessary concession to the critics of Economics. On the main point under discussion, however, I have nothing to retract, and in what follows I have borrowed one or two sentences from the last few paragraphs of the article.

[2] On all this it seems to me that the elucidations of Max Weber are quite definitive. Indeed, I confess that I am quite unable to understand how it can be conceived to be possible to call this part of Max Weber's methodology in question. (See *Der Sinn der "Wertfreiheit" der Soziologischen und Ökonomischen Wissenschaften. Gesammelte Aufsätze zur Wissenschaftslehre*, pp. 451-502.)

is a proposition which we cannot conceive being
verified at all in this manner. Propositions involving
the verb "ought" are different in kind from propositions involving the verb "is". And it is difficult to see
what possible good can be served by not keeping them
separate, or failing to recognise their essential difference.[1]

All this is not to say that economists may not
assume as postulates different judgments of value,
and then on the assumption that these are valid enquire
what judgment is to be passed upon particular pro-
posals for action. On the contrary, as we shall see, it
is just in the light that it casts upon the significance
and consistency of different ultimate valuations that
the utility of Economics consists. Applied Economics
consists of propositions of the form, "If you want to
do this, then you must do that." "If such and such is
to be regarded as the ultimate good, then this is clearly
incompatible with it." All that is implied in the distinction here emphasised is that the validity of assumptions
relating to the value of what exists or what may exist
is not a matter of scientific verification, as is the validity
of assumptions relating to mere existence.

Nor is it in the least implied that economists should
not deliver themselves on ethical questions, any more
than an argument that botany is not æsthetics is to

[1] Mr. J. A. Hobson, commenting on a passage in my criticism of Mr.
Hawtrey which was couched in somewhat similar terms, protests that
"this is a refusal to recognise any empirical *modus vivendi* or contact between
economic values and human values" (Hobson, *op. cit.*, p. 129). Precisely,
but why should Mr. Hobson, of all men, complain? My procedure simply
empties out of Economics—what Mr. Hobson himself has never ceased to
proclaim to be an illegitimate intrusion—any "economic" presumption that
the valuations of the market-place are ethically respectable. I cannot help
feeling that a great many of Mr. Hobson's strictures on the procedure of
Economic Science fall to the ground if the view of the scope of its subject-
matter suggested above be explicitly adopted.

say that botanists should not have views of their own
on the lay-out of gardens. On the contrary, it is
greatly to be desired that economists should have
speculated long and widely on these matters, since
only in this way will they be in a position to appreciate the implications as regards *given* ends of problems
which are put to them for solution. We may not
agree with J. S. Mill that "a man is not likely to be
a good economist if he is nothing else." But we may
at least agree that he may not be as useful as he otherwise might be. Our methodological axioms involve
no prohibition of outside interests! All that is contended is that there is no logical connection between
the two types of generalisation, and that there is
nothing to be gained by invoking the sanctions of one
to reinforce the conclusions of the other.

And, quite apart from all questions of methodology,
there is a very practical justification for such a procedure. In the rough-and-tumble of political struggle,
differences of opinion may arise either as a result of
differences about ends or as a result of differences
about the means of attaining ends. Now, as regards
the first type of difference, neither Economics nor any
other science can provide any solvent. If we disagree
about ends it is a case of thy blood or mine—or live
and let live, according to the importance of the difference, or the relative strength of our opponents. But,
if we disagree about means, then scientific analysis
can often help us to resolve our differences. If we disagree about the morality of the taking of interest (and
we understand what we are talking about),[1] then there
is no room for argument. But if we disagree about the
objective implications of fluctuations in the rate of

[1] See below, Section 5.

interest, then economic analysis should enable us to settle our dispute. Shut Mr. Hawtrey in a room as Secretary of a Committee composed of Bentham, Buddha, Lenin and the Head of the United States Steel Corporation, set up to decide upon the ethics of usury, and it is improbable that he could produce an "agreed document". Set the same committee to determine the objective results of State regulation of the rate of discount, and it ought not to be beyond human ingenuity to produce unanimity—or at any rate a majority report, with Lenin perhaps dissenting. Surely, for the sake of securing what agreement we can in a world in which avoidable differences of opinion are all too common, it is worth while carefully delimiting those fields of enquiry where this kind of settlement is possible from those where it is not to be hoped for[1]—it is worth while delimiting the neutral area of science from the more disputable area of moral and political philosophy.

5. But what, then, is the significance of Economic

---

[1] In fact, of course, such has been the practice of economists of the "orthodox" tradition ever since the emergence of scientific economics. See, e.g., Cantillon, *Essai sur la Nature du Commerce* (Higgs' ed., p. 85): "It is also a question outside of my subject whether it is better to have a great multitude of inhabitants poor and badly provided, than a smaller number much more at their ease". See also Ricardo, *Notes on Malthus*, p. 188: "It has been well said by M. Say that it is not the province of the Political Economist to advise—he is to tell you how you may become rich, but he is not to advise you to prefer riches to indolence or indolence to riches". Of course, occasionally among those economists who have worked with a hedonistic bias, there has been confusion of the two kinds of proposition. But this has not happened to anything like the extent commonly suggested. Most of the allegations of bias spring from unwillingness to believe the facts that economic analysis brings to light. The proposition that real wages above the equilibrium point involve unemployment is a perfectly neutral inference from one of the most elementary propositions in theoretical economics. But it is difficult to mention it in some circles without being accused, if not of sinister interest, at least of a hopeless bias against the poor and the unfortunate. Similarly at the present day it is difficult to enunciate the platitude that a general tariff on imports will affect foreign demand for our exports without being thought a traitor to one's country.

Science? We have seen that it provides, within its own structure of generalisations, no norms which are binding in practice. It is incapable of deciding as between the desirability of different ends. It is fundamentally distinct from Ethics. Wherein, then, does its unquestionable significance consist?

Surely it consists in just this, that, when we are faced with a choice between ultimates, it enables us to choose with full awareness of the implications of what we are choosing. Faced with the problem of deciding between this and that, we are not entitled to look to Economics for the ultimate decision. There is nothing in Economics which relieves *us* of the obligation to choose. There is nothing in any kind of science which can decide the ultimate problem of preference. But, to be completely rational, we must know what it is we prefer. We must be aware of the implications of the alternatives. For rationality in choice is nothing more and nothing less than choice with complete awareness of the alternatives rejected. And it is just here that Economics acquires its practical significance. It can make clear to us the implications of the different ends we may choose. It makes it possible for us to will with knowledge of what it is we are willing. It makes it possible for us to select a system of ends which are mutually consistent with each other.[1]

An example or two should make this quite clear. Let us start with a case in which the implications of

---

[1] It is perhaps desirable to emphasise that the consistency which is made possible is a consistency of achievement, not a consistency of ends. The achievement of one end may be held to be inconsistent with the achievement of another, either on the plane of valuation, or on the plane of objective possibility. Thus it may be held to be ethically inconsistent to serve two masters at once. It is objectively inconsistent to arrange to be with each of them at the same time, at different places. It is the latter kind of inconsistency in the sphere of social policy which scientific Economics should make it possible to eliminate.

one act of choice are elucidated. We may revert once more to an example we have already considered—the imposition of a protective tariff. We have seen already that there is nothing in scientific Economics which warrants our describing such a policy as good or bad. We have decided that, if such a policy is decided upon with full consciousness of the sacrifices involved, there is no justification for describing it as uneconomical. The deliberate choice by a body of citizens acting collectively to frustrate, in the interests of ends such as defence, the preservation of the countryside, and so on, their several choices as consumers, cannot be described as uneconomical or irrational, if it is done with full awareness of what is being done. But this will not be the case unless the citizens in question are fully conscious of the objective implications of the step they are taking. And in an extensive modern society it is only as a result of intricate economic analysis that they may be placed in possession of this knowledge. The great majority, even of educated people, called upon to decide upon the desirability of, let us say, protection for agriculture, think only of the effects of such measures on the protected industry. They see that such measures are likely to benefit the industry, and hence they argue that the measures are good. But, of course, as every first year student knows, it is only here that the problem begins. To judge the further repercussions of the tariff an analytical technique is necessary. This is why in countries where the level of education in Economics is not high, there is a constant tendency to the approval of more and more protective tariffs.

Nor is the utility of such analysis to be regarded as confined to decisions on isolated measures such as the imposition of a single tariff. It enables us to judge more complicated systems of policy. It enables us to see what *sets* of ends are compatible with each other and what are not, and upon what conditions such compatibility is dependent. And, indeed, it is just here that the possession of some such technique becomes quite indispensable if policy is to be rational. It may be just possible to will rationally the achievement of particular social ends overriding individual valuations without much assistance from analysis. The case of a subsidy to protect essential food supplies is a case in point. It is almost impossible to conceive the carrying through of more elaborate policies without the aid of such an instrument.[1]

We may take an example from the sphere of monetary policy. It is an unescapable deduction from the first principles of monetary theory that, in a world in which conditions are changing at different rates in different monetary areas, it is impossible to achieve at once stable prices and stable exchanges.[2] The two ends—in this case the "ends" are quite obviously subordinate to other major norms of policy—are logically incompatible. You may try for one or you may try for the other—it is not certain that price stability is either permanently attainable or conducive to equili-

---

[1] All this should be a sufficient answer to those who continually lay it down that "social life is too complex a matter to be judged by economic analysis". It is because social life is so complicated that economic analysis is necessary if we are to understand even a part of it. It is usually those who talk most about the complexity of life and the insusceptibility of human behaviour to any kind of logical analysis who prove to have the most *simpliste* intellectual and emotional make-up. He who has really glimpsed the irrational in the springs of human action will have no "fear" that it can ever be killed by logic.

[2] See Keynes, *A Tract on Monetary Reform*, pp. 154-155; also an interesting paper by Mr. D. H. Robertson, *How do We Want Gold to Behave?* reprinted in the *International Gold Problem*, pp. 18-46.

brium generally—but you cannot rationally try for both. If you do, there must be a breakdown. These conclusions are well known to all economists. Yet without some analytical apparatus how few of us would perceive the incompatibility of the ends in question!

And even this is a narrow example. Without economic analysis it is not possible rationally to choose between alternative *systems* of society. We have seen already that if we regard a society which permits inequality of incomes as an evil in itself, and an equalitarian society as presenting an end to be pursued above all other things, then it is illegitimate to regard such a preference as uneconomic. But it is not possible to regard it as rational unless it is formulated with a full consciousness of the nature of the sacrifice which is thereby involved. And we cannot do this unless we understand, not only the essential nature of the capitalistic mechanism, but also the necessary conditions and limitations to which the type of society proposed as a substitute would be subject. It is not rational to will a certain end if one is not conscious of what sacrifice the achievement of that end involves. And, in this supreme weighing of alternatives, only a complete awareness of the implications of modern economic analysis can confer the capacity to judge rationally.

But, if this is so, what need is there to claim any larger status for Economic Science? Is it not the burden of our time that we do not realise what we are doing? Are not most of our difficulties due to just this fact, that we will ends which are incompatible, not because we wish for deadlock, but because we do not realise their incompatibility. It may well be that there

may exist; differences as regards ultimate ends in
modern society which render some conflict inevitable.
But it is clear that many of our most pressing difficulties arise, not for this reason, but because our aims
are not co-ordinated. As consumers we will cheapness,
as producers we choose security. We value one distribution of factors of production as private spenders
and savers. As public citizens we sanction arrangements which frustrate the achievement of this distribution. We call for cheap money and lower prices,
fewer imports and a larger volume of trade.[1] The
different "will-organisations" in society, although
composed of the same individuals, formulate different
preferences. Everywhere our difficulties seem to
arise, not so much from divisions between the
different members of the body politic, as from, as
it were, split personalities on the part of each one
of them.[2]

To such a situation, Economics brings the solvent
of knowledge. It enables us to conceive the far-
reaching implications of alternative possibilities of
policy. It does not, and it cannot, enable us to evade
the necessity of choosing between alternatives. But
it does make it possible for us to bring our different
choices into harmony. It cannot remove the ultimate
limitations on human action. But it does make it
possible within these limitations to act consistently.
It serves for the inhabitant of the modern world with
its endless interconnections and relationships as an

[1] *Cf.* M. S. Braun, *Theorie der Staatlichen Wirtschaftspolitik*, p. 5.

[2] In this way economic analysis reveals still further examples of a
phenomenon to which attention has often been drawn in recent discussion
of the theory of Sovereignty in Public Law. See Figgis, *Churches in the
Modern State*; Maitland, *Introduction to* Gierke's *Political Theories of the
Middle Ages*; Laski, *The Problem of Sovereignty, Authority in the Modern
State*.

extension of his perceptive apparatus. It provides a technique of rational action.

This, then, is a further sense in which Economics can be truly said to assume rationality in human society. It makes no pretence, as has been alleged so often, that action is necessarily rational in the sense that the ends pursued are not mutually inconsistent. There is nothing in its generalisations which necessarily implies reflective deliberation in ultimate valuation. It relies upon no assumption that individuals will always act rationally. But it does depend for its practical *raison d'être* upon the assumption that it is desirable that they should do so. It does assume that, within the bounds of necessity, it is desirable to choose ends which can be achieved harmoniously.

And thus in the last analysis Economics does depend, if not for its existence, at least for its significance, on an ultimate valuation—the affirmation that rationality and ability to choose with knowledge is desirable. If irrationality, if the surrender to the blind force of external stimuli and unco-ordinated impulse at every moment is a good to be preferred above all others, then it is true the *raison d'être* of Economics disappears. And it is the tragedy of our generation, red with fratricidal strife and betrayed almost beyond belief by those who should have been its intellectual leaders, that there have arisen those who would uphold this ultimate negation, this escape from the tragic necessities of choice which has become conscious. With all such there can be no argument. The revolt against reason is essentially a revolt against life itself. But for all those who still affirm more positive values, that branch of knowledge which, above all others, is the symbol and safeguard of rationality in social arrangements, must, in the anxious days which are to come, by very reason of this menace to that for which it stands, possess a peculiar and a heightened significance.

INDEX OF AUTHORS CITED

Printed in Great Britain by
Billing and Sons Ltd., Guildford and Esher
03967